Mike and Phani's Essential C++ Techniques

MICHAEL HYMAN
AND
PHANI VADDADI

Mike and Phani's Essential C++ Techniques
Copyright ©1999 by Michael Hyman and Phani Vaddadi

Library of Congress Cataloging-in-Publication Data
    Hyman, Michael I., 1965–
        Mike and Phani's Essential C++ Techniques / Michael Hyman &
        Phani Vaddadi
            p.   cm.
        1. C++ (Computer program language)   I. Vaddadi, Phani, 1959–
    II. Title.
    QA76.73.C153H962   1999
    005.1313—dc21   99-38901
                                                                        CIP

ISBN (pbk): 1-893115-04-6
Printed and bound in the United States of America
1 2 3 4 5 6 7 8 9 10

Trademarked names may appear in this book. Rather than use a trademark symbol with every occurrence of a trademarked name, we use the names only in an editorial fashion and to the benefit of the trademark owner, with no intention of infringement of the trademark.

Project Manager: Nancy DelFavero
Technical Reviewer: Thomas Olsen
Editorial Services and Page Composition: Impressions Book and
    Journal Services, Inc.
Copy Editor: Ann Edahl
Indexer: Nina Forrest
Cover and Interior Design: Derek Yee Design

Distributed to the book trade worldwide by Springer-Verlag New York, Inc.
175 Fifth Avenue, New York, NY 10010
In the United States, phone 1-800-SPRINGER; orders@springer-ny.com
http://www.springer-ny.com

For information on translations, please contact APress directly:
APress, 6400 Hollis Street, Suite 9, Emeryville, CA 94608
Phone: 510/595-3110; Fax: 510/595-3122; info@apress.com; www.apress.com

The information in this book is distributed on an "As Is" basis, without warranty. Although every precaution has been taken in the preparation of this work, neither the author nor APress shall have any liability to any person or entity with respect to any loss or damage caused or alleged to be caused directly or indirectly by the information contained in this work.

Dedication

To Miriam and Pooja, and Seeta and Sarah

Authors' Acknowledgments

Michael says: Writing a book is like swimming deep under water. You don't always know where you're going. It's a struggle and there's a lot of pressure. But if you somehow manage to swim toward the light, you know you'll be able to breath again. So I'd like to thank all of those who helped provide some light. First, to Phani for his hard work as we crafted this book together. I learned a lot and it was a pleasure. To Thomas Olsen for his excellent work as a tech editor. To Simon Bernstein for his backup tech edits. To the folks at APress, especially Gary Cornell for believing in this book and making writing it fun (you know what I mean) and Nancy DelFavero for all her hard work shepherding it through. Thanks to the folks at Impressions for slogging through it so many times to make it better and Ann Edahl for copyediting the text. Finally, of course, I'd like to thank my family. You are always the victims of any endeavor such as this. Thanks for putting up with me during all the times when I disappeared into the basement bowing to the silicon god.

Phani says: Many authors have told me that writing a book is a difficult, worthless venture. Despite those warnings, I let Mike persuade me to write this one with him. Well, they are all wrong. It's a great experience and such a pleasant one at that. Maybe I just lucked out to find smart people who are also easy to work with. I would like to express my thanks to the following. First, Mike for convincing me that what we do as routine practice is worth writing about. It's also a real pleasure to see how he makes it seem easy to write about stuff. Thomas Olsen for providing useful and excellent technical feedback on the book and code. Simon Bernstein for providing the extra pair of eyes to review the code. Gary Cornell, Nancy DelFavero, and the others at APress. They proved that APress does indeed provide an author-friendly environment. Thanks also to the people at Impressions for their editing and production work. Thanks to my family who tolerated all those times when I would disappear into a dark place and work on my computer when I should have been out enjoying the sun. And special thanks to Dusty, my daughter's dog, for being by my side during late-night coding sessions, telling me in his silent way that there is more to life than programming.

About the Authors

Michael Hyman is the author of ten other computer books, including *Visual C++ For Dummies, Dynamic HTML For Dummies,* and *PC Roadkill.* He was a columnist for *Microsoft Interactive Developer* and for *Windows Tech Journal.* He has worked on operating systems, compilers, databases, and interactive television. He currently works on multimedia technology for a large software company in the northwest. He has an Electrical Engineering and Computer Science degree from Princeton University.

Phani Vaddadi has ten years experience as a development manager at a major software company. He has worked on office products, Internet multimedia authoring and runtimes, and Internet commerce and database technology. He has built and managed numerous development teams and has also managed program management and test organizations. He ran development at a CAD start-up, worked on computer vision, and has experience in the atomic energy industry. He has a degree in Electrical Engineering from Andhra University.

Contents

Chapter 3 Dealing with Compiler-Generated Code 37

Chapter 4 Pointers and Memory 43

Chapter 16 Specific Debugging Stuff

Part II Sample Code

Introduction

WELCOME. AT THIS POINT, YOU PROBABLY HAVE A FEW QUESTIONS: Why should I buy this book? How does it work? Why the heck should I trust you anyway?

You should buy this book for one reason: to improve your coding skills. Now, we're not going to pretend that we are the best programmers on the planet. Nor are we going to claim that every page in this book will be packed with revelations so deep that you'll feel that lightning has struck. But we will tell you that we have condensed lessons into this book learned from a heck of a lot of time spent writing code and creating products.

Some of the techniques you'll find may seem like common sense. Duh, you'll say. Others will reveal tricks you haven't imagined. In either case, we tried to write the kind of book that we've wished for—one with lots of information, lots of code, and not so many words that you'll doze off. A book that you can pick up, flip to any random page, and learn something.

We've organized the book into two parts:

Part I has all of the guts. It's broken into chapters that deal with key programming concepts, such as using classes, optimizing code, and dealing with pointers. Each of these chapters is composed of techniques. The techniques have categories, some sample code—often showing before-and-after code—and a brief discussion of the advantages of employing each technique. For some techniques, we refer to examples; those sample files can be found on this book's accompanying CD-ROM. You can focus on chapters relating to a topic you want to learn more about, or you can read through the book at random, using your favorite page traversal algorithm to decide what to look at or look up.

Part II lists most of the sample code we created for illustrating the techniques in Part I. You'll find code for manipulating strings, performing regular expression matches, handling dynamic arrays, and performing reference counting. As with the techniques in Part I, we show mostly code along with a brief explanation of why the code does what it does. You can find the complete sample files on the accompanying CD-ROM. The appendix to this book explains how to go about using the disc.

Why should you trust us? Well, to start, we're not politicians. We don't sell used cars. (Although, now that you mention it, if you're looking for a '65 Dodge Dart . . .) More important, we've had a lot of experience shipping products. Chances are extremely high, in fact, that some code that we've written is on your very own machine. We've worked for start-ups and large software companies, on products ranging from databases to operating systems, from CAD software to

Internet runtimes. In this book, we share some of the lessons we've learned in the process. Things to avoid. Ways to write tighter code. And the important stuff, like that cold pizza is perfectly fine for breakfast.

In short, buy this book. Use this book. Tell your friends about it. Visit us at www.essentialtechniques.com and drop us a line, letting us know what you think. Heck, even tell us your favorite techniques or send us requests on techniques you'd like us to write about in the future. Then, loosen up your fingers and get back to work.

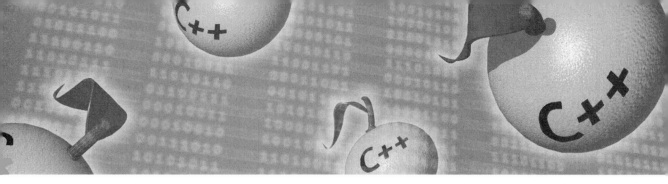

Part I

The Techniques

WELCOME TO PART I. HERE YOU'LL FIND CHAPTER AFTER CHAPTER full of techniques to improve your coding skills. Some of the techniques are simple advice, such as how to think about problems. Others go through the gory details, such as walking the stack frame when debugging.

Although the techniques are grouped together into chapters that focus on specific areas, such as memory allocation or performance, there is no need to read the chapters sequentially. You can simply jump from technique to technique. Each technique stands on its own. You can pick up the book and put it down whenever you need to. (Heck, you can think of it as the perfect book to keep stashed in the bathroom. Your guests will love it.)

The techniques all follow a similar layout. You'll get the title of the technique, a category for it, and then code (in most cases) and an explanation. Some techniques refer to the sample code that comes on this book's companion CD-ROM, and may also have cross-references or caveats.

The categories help you understand the basic goal of the technique. You'll find the following category types, and their respective meanings, noted with the techniques listed in Part I:

Advice: A general technique, usually focused on a practice more than a specific coding approach. Sometimes these are philosophical or management related.

Avoid crashes: A technique that will help prevent crashes, such as relating to null pointers. Such techniques often help avoid unexpected results as well.

Avoid hard-to-find problems: A technique that will save a lot of head scratching and debugging time.

Avoid memory leaks: A technique aimed at preventing memory loss and eventual performance degradation.

Avoid stupid mistakes: A technique for avoiding those embarrassing moments when nothing works but the problem is immediately obvious to anyone else who looks at the code.

Avoid unexpected results: A technique that will help you write code that does what you think it should. Many of these help prevent subtle, pain-in-the-rear bugs.

Compile your code: A technique relating to some subtlety of C++ syntax bound to keep your code from compiling.

How to: A technique explaining how to do something, such as how to walk a stack frame while debugging.

Workaround: A technique to help you get around, how shall we say it, behavioral inconsistencies?

Write cleaner code: A technique for improving your coding style.

Write faster code: A technique for improving the speed of your code.

Write maintainable code: A technique for improving your coding style, usually by making your code easier to read and understand.

Write more efficient code: A technique for reducing code size or repetition.

CHAPTER 1
Start with a Good Design

THIS CHAPTER DISCUSSES GENERAL TECHNIQUES related to programming. None of these involve code. Rather, they provide advice for dealing with the processes and problems of creating and shipping products. As you read through these techniques, you might say to yourself, "Thanks a lot for the advice, guys. It sounds good on paper. Too bad you don't understand what *I'm* going through." But that's exactly the point of these techniques. We do understand what you're going through. We've shipped a lot of products under a lot of circumstances. We know all too well what it is like to be coding at two in the morning, week after week, to meet an impossible deadline. We've worked in both dysfunctional and smoothly operating teams. So although sometimes these tips may sound wishy-washy, they really do work.

If, however, you want to dig right into some coding techniques, skip this chapter and move on to Chapter 2.

Technique 1: Define the Problem

Category: Advice

It is hard to solve a problem if you don't know what the problem is. Ask yourself the following questions:

- What are you creating?

- Why are you creating it?

- How are you going to create it?

- What is the user going to experience?

- What are the boundaries?

- What are the assumptions?

- What are the requirements?

- When do you need to finish?

- How will you know if you are successful?

Technique 2: Use the 1-3-5 Rule

Category: Advice

A successful project should have one mission, three targeted customers, and no more than five benefits: 1-3-5. This is a rule we've invented, so spread the word.

If you want your project to be successful, it should have one mission, and everyone on the team should understand and agree on the mission. The mission shouldn't be so nebulous that anything could be part of it. (For example, "Build great software" is a crummy mission; "Create the smallest, fastest Internet browser" is okay.) If you have more than one mission, you'll never know when to stop.

You should identify no more than three customers to target. This doesn't mean that you shouldn't have any more than three customers. Instead, it means that you should categorize your customers into no more than three buckets. Then pick the prototypical customer from each bucket. Those are the folks you should talk to for getting your key advice and for targeting your feature set. If you have too many customers, you'll have feature creep. You won't know which features are more important than others. You'll try to do them all. Your management will jerk you around.

Finally, have no more than five benefits. That is all a customer can remember anyway. This doesn't mean you shouldn't have more than five features. But these features should all work together to provide some benefit to the customer. You don't need a million features to make a product successful. If you have a million features, they will be buggy, your product will be huge, and the customer won't have a clue how to use them anyway. Keep things smaller and more focused. The rest of the features can wait until the next release.

Technique 3: Solution in Search of a Problem

Category: Advice

Before you begin coding, you need to understand your group's situation. If you have thought of some really cool technology and just need to make sure that the world learns about it, you may be in trouble. Take a step back.

- Determine if there really is a problem at hand or if you are just doing technology for technology's sake.

- Determine if there is a target customer that can at least help you make design trade-offs or determine when your project is finished.

If you can't identify a customer, or if you keep coming back to a mission of completely *changing the world*, be careful. You may find it hard to define goals, make trade-offs, and define milestones. You may find that your project will only flourish to the extent it is either undiscovered or protected by a specific manager. You may also find that, after you have completed your brilliant work, no one will use it and it (and perhaps you) end up shelved.

Caveat

If your job is basic research, this rule may not apply. Or you may be able to avoid the inevitable for a longer period of time.

Technique 4: Problem in Search of a Solution

Category: Advice

If you have identified a customer or future problem and are trying to find a solution, you are in great shape.

- Refer to the customer needs when you need to make design trade-offs.

- Identify the key parts of the problem that you will solve.

- Identify what you will not solve. Don't be wimpy and pretend you will solve everything; save yourself a headache and plan out what you won't do up front.

- Understand how you differ from other solutions.

- Then go solve the problem.

Technique 5: In Search of a Solution and Problem

Category: Advice

If you have a bunch of cool people who want to get together and do something cool, you are halfway there. After all, it can be hard to build a team. But you had better figure out what you are doing and why.

If you have a task at hand but aren't quite sure who the customer is, and you aren't quite sure what solution to use, or which of several approaches make sense, and really, why you are even bothering, look out. Then polish your résumé.

Technique 6: KISS—Keep It Simple and Stupid

Category: Advice

Complex designs don't make you more impressive. They just make you more error prone. Try to come up with the simplest solution for the problem at hand. Often the simple solutions will be easier to code and thus have fewer bugs. They will have fewer code paths and thus will be easier to test. They will be easier to optimize and thus will be faster.

Now, this doesn't mean that you should sacrifice efficiency for simplicity. For example, if you know that one design's performance will degrade geometrically and the other will degrade linearly, certainly go for the better performing design—but only if you'll see the degradation when customers are using it. ("But, but," you say, "if two million people logged on to my machine on my modem . . .")

Think carefully about your design. If you make a design that is so complex that only you can understand it, you'll only end up impressing yourself. Everyone else will be confused or wonder why you didn't use a simpler approach.

Caveat

If you want to lock customers into using your product and no one else's, make the interfaces so complex that, once they finish learning how to use your product, there won't be any more room in their brain for learning anything else. Oh wait, did I get cynical for a moment?

Technique 7: The Importance of Good Design

Category: Advice

Optimize before you start coding. You can create all the hand-tuned assembly code you want, but such optimizations will never give you the same benefits as a good design. A properly chosen algorithm will always give you bigger performance, and stability wins.

- Understand the problem before you design.

- Design to the problem.

- Think about future directions and generalize where it makes sense. But don't overgeneralize to the point that you solve some huge imaginary problem but don't do such a good job with the problem at hand.

Technique 8: The Customer Is Always Right

Category: Advice

This is a problem that often plagues projects. It is also related to other techniques in this chapter. Don't sell the customer the idea that they need your technology. Sell them the idea that your solution solves their problem. The way to do this is to start by understanding their needs. Solve their problems. Don't solve a theoretical problem and then look for someone who needs the technology.

If the customer tells you that your solution doesn't work, fix it. Don't argue with them about why they are stupid and don't understand your brilliance.

Caveat

Sometimes they *are* stupid and don't understand your brilliance, in which case you may need to change your message.

Technique 9: Design Is an Iterative Process

Category: Advice

You are not going to get it right the first time. Don't be afraid to redesign. After you have gone through the exercise of your first design, analyze it. Think about it. Review it with others. Figure out how to improve it. Most projects get redesigned three times before they ship.

Your design will also change throughout the project in response to customer feedback and as you discover more of the details and "gotchas" of your problem. That is good.

Technique 10: Coding Is Also an Iterative Process

Category: Advice

You are not going to get it right the first time. It is okay to recode. It is okay to think about ways that you can reuse code that you, or other people, have written or ways that you can apply your techniques to a broader problem. It is also okay to discover that you screwed up in some of your assumptions and that you need to start over again. (But after the fifth time blundering on the same problem, you might want to get a little help. Or consider becoming a politician.)

Technique 11: Work Smarter, Not Longer

Category: Advice

It is hard to program when you are asleep.

Programmers are stubborn and obsessive by nature. When confronted with a task and a deadline, we naturally tend to work extremely long hours to complete the task. Unfortunately, we really are mere mortals. (I promise I won't tell anyone.) Lack of sleep can cause decreased attention span, temper flares, and general slop.

When you are tired, you tend to take longer to accomplish tasks, and you introduce more bugs. Take a break. Get some sleep. Give your brain a rest. When you return to your task, you will likely be far more efficient.

Unfortunately, it is often difficult to recognize when you are in this state. It helps to have coworkers, a manager, or friends who can pull you out of the stress-filled drive and tell you to relax a little. Listen to them.

Caveat

Sometimes you have to ignore this advice and just ship the damn thing—but be very wary of increased bug count and bug regressions.

Technique 12: Four Eyes Are Better than Two

Category: Advice

No matter how good a programmer you are, you are bound to make mistakes. If you can't come up with a clean design for a problem, discuss it with coworkers. They may have a different approach or thought process that can unblock you. Think of it as small-scope brainstorming.

If you haven't had much sleep or are stressed out because of deadlines, ask others to look over your work.

Be sure to review your designs and your code with peers. They can help you uncover bugs and potential problems and may suggest other solutions. The process of review can help everyone on the team improve their skills.

A nice side effect of reviewing is that the team gains a broader understanding of the designs and code on the project. This in turn makes it easier for team members to see the big picture and pitch in when needed.

Technique 13: Measure Twice, Cut Once

Category: Advice

Fix your problems before you create them. Work through all of the issues during your design phase. After you design, go back and see if it really met your design needs. See if you can simplify it. See if it scales. It is much easier to create a good design if you haven't already invested loads of time chasing after a bad one. See if there are other solutions similar to what you are trying to do. Read.

In other words, don't be in a hurry to code.

Technique 14: Know When to Say When

Category: Advice

Don't overdesign. Can you simplify what you are doing? Can you generalize? Can you find a cleaner approach? I've seen plenty of simple software become extremely complex in a hurry, as alternate syntax, garbage collection, fancy memory allocators, complex timing loops, and so on were added. The end result is usually a huge mess that may or may not work. Quite often, all of the techniques that are good in isolation don't make your product any faster or better.

Simpler designs are easier to implement, track, and tune. Simplicity many times also leads to speed: your code will have a smaller working set and you'll have a better clue as to what it is actually doing.

Do the right amount of design and coding to get the problem solved.

Technique 15: Pick the Right Algorithm and Data Structures for the Problem

Category: Advice

Good algorithms and data structures make good programs. Don't choose the most complex data structure in the world to prove what a hot shot you are. Choose it if it solves the problem the best way. Likewise, don't use arrays for everything just because you are scared of screwing up if you write something more complex.

Figure out what meets the needs. Ask around. Read. Talk it over. Experiment. Write small isolated programs to test out the concept, algorithm, or new data structure. When you feel comfortable, use it in your work.

Good algorithms and data structures make efficient programs. You'll get more benefit from good algorithms than you will from extensive code tuning or rewriting your code in assembly language.

Understand the data that you are manipulating. If you understand the data, you are 90 percent on the way to understanding the problem.

Here are some things you should ask:

- What are the storage implications?

- What are the insert, delete, and seek implications?

- What are the use patterns? Let them dictate your needs.

- How will the program need to grow in the future?

- How will the program need to scale?

CHAPTER 2

Darn Reasonable Practices

I'M SICK OF THE TERM *BEST PRACTICES*. I have no clue what it means, outside of it being a nice-sounding buzzword for attracting people to seminars. This chapter instead focuses on some *darn reasonable* practices. These practices don't concentrate on any specific area but, rather, cover the gamut of programming.

As promised in the introduction to this book, this chapter and most of those that follow are primarily code with a little bit of yakking thrown in.

Technique 16: Be Careful When Cutting and Pasting Code

Category: Avoid stupid mistakes

Before

```
if (m_lpBuffer)
   GlobalFree(m_lpBuffer);
if (m_lpScreen)
   GlobalFree(m_lpBuffer);
```

After

```
if (m_lpBuffer)
   GlobalFree(m_lpBuffer);
if (m_lpScreen)
   GlobalFree(m_lpScreen);
```

When you are programming, you probably cut and paste code to save typing time. When doing so, make sure that you properly update the code that you've pasted. In the "Before" code listed in this section, we've taken a line for freeing a pointer and copied it. You can see that, although we changed the variable name used in the conditional, we forgot to change the variable name that we actually free. This oversight will lead to some unpleasant side effects. It is often hard to find these bugs because if you glance over the code rather than carefully examining it, it might look okay.

Although this particular example is simple, in real life cut-and-paste bugs can be more complex. Be particularly careful when copying classes and functions. The compiler will coerce arguments when it can, and you may find that you have an overloaded operator that can be coerced to, but doesn't, do what you expected.

Single-stepping over the code in the debugger will usually reveal these kinds of bugs. Always single-step in the debugger over every new line of code you write before you ship the product (see Technique 138).

With the "Before" example shown for this technique, you'll catch the incorrect delete in the debugger when you crash.

The following incorrect code, however, won't crash. Instead, it will leak memory if m_lpBuffer is null. You may not catch it when you run your program (see Technique 62), but you will catch it if you carefully step through your code in the debugger:

```
if(m_lpBuffer)
    delete m_lpBuffer;
if(m_lpBuffer)
    delete m_lpscreen;
```

Technique 17: Initialize Local Variables

Category: Avoid stupid mistakes

Before

```
int SArray::IndexFind(long l)
{
    int iLeft;
    int iRight;
    int iMiddle;
    long lM;

    if(m_clMac == 0)
        return 0;

    while(iLeft < iRight)
    {
        iMiddle = (iLeft + iRight)/2;
```

After

```
int SArray::IndexFind(long l)
{
    int iLeft = 0;
    int iRight = m_clMac;
    int iMiddle;
    long lM;

    if(m_clMac == 0)
        return 0;

    while(iLeft < iRight)
    {
        iMiddle = (iLeft + iRight)/2;
```

It's easy to forget to initialize local variables. After all, it does seem like such a mundane chore. Plus, in many cases you know darn well that you are going to calculate the value anyway. For example, in the "Before" code for this technique, the value of iMiddle is always calculated before it is used.

On the other hand, iLeft and iRight are not calculated before they are used. As a result, if you forget to initialize their values, you'll get all types of unexpected results. In this case, the loop could terminate unexpectedly.

Have the discipline to initialize all local variables before you use them. (The compiler will often warn you if you don't. Compilers such as Microsoft Visual C++ generally detect uses of uninitialized pointers.)

See example: bsrch.cpp

Technique 18: Validate Arguments

Category: Avoid crashes and unexpected results

Before

```
BOOL BF::Get(int ibit)
{
```

After

```
BOOL BF::Get(int ibit)
{
    if(ibit >= m_cbit || ibit < 0)
    return(FALSE);
```

Users don't read manuals. You can't expect that values passed in to member functions—and especially to public member functions—will be in the correct range.

Check the values of arguments and user input before you process them. If a value exceeds the acceptable range, either clip it (set it to the minimum or maximum acceptable value), set it to a default value, return from the function with an error code, or throw an exception.

Remember to check the top and bottom of the range.

See example: BF::Get() in bits.cpp

Technique 19: Check Return Codes

Category: Avoid crashes

Before

```
BOOL  BF::FSetSize(DWORD cbitNeeded)
{
    DWORD *pdw;
    long cdw;

    cdw = (cbitNeeded + cbitDWORD - 1)/ cbitDWORD;
    pdw = new DWORD[cdw];
    memset(pdw, 0L, sizeof(DWORD) * cdw);
```

After

```
BOOL  BF::FSetSize(DWORD cbitNeeded)
{
    DWORD *pdw;
    long cdw;

    cdw = (cbitNeeded + cbitDWORD - 1)/ cbitDWORD;
    pdw = new DWORD[cdw];
    if(pdw)
    {
        memset(pdw, 0L, sizeof(DWORD) * cdw);
```

You might think that library functions always succeed. Well, surprise. They don't. In the sample code just listed, you can see that the "Before" example assumes that the memory allocation succeeds. But what happens if it doesn't? Kaboom. What else did you expect?

Check the return codes from library functions, especially those that need to allocate resources, such as memory, file, and network operations.

Caveat

You don't need to go overboard with this. You actually only need to check return codes if a failure matters to you. For example, if you are drawing a bunch of lines to the screen and don't care if one of the draws doesn't occur, then you don't need to check the return code. When in doubt, err on the side of caution.

As always, expect that memory allocations will fail and guard your code for such a case. It is a good practice to separate your code into (1) functions that require user validation and (2) functions that don't require validation for perf reasons. But always guard your assumptions with asserts just in case—even when you don't think you need to validate parameters.

See example: `BF::FSetSize()` in bits.cpp

Technique 20: Check for 0 before Dividing

Category: Avoid crashes

Before

```
nRes = nNum / nDenom;
```

After

```
if (nDenom)
    nRes = nNum / nDenom;
else
    //Supply some default result here
    nRes = 0;
```

If you divide by zero, you'll generate a runtime error or exception. Usually, this error will be passed on to the user just before your program crashes. Whenever you divide by a variable (or calculated value), check for zero if there is a chance that the denominator could be zero.

Having a divide-by-zero may also expose a bad design problem. Check that, too. Just fixing the error locally could hide a more fundamental problem. First convince yourself that it is okay for the denominator to be zero. (Did you scratch your head when you found this problem, wondering why it occurred?) If you didn't expect that the denominator could be zero, examine your design carefully. You may have a lot more work to do. If, on the other hand, it really is okay for the denominator to be zero, go ahead and fix the bug by protecting yourself as shown in this example.

Technique 21: Check for 0 before Mod'ing

Category: Avoid crashes

Before

```
nRes = 13 % nMod;
```

After

```
if (nMod)
    nRes = 13 % nMod;
else
    //Supply some default result here
    nRes = 0;
```

This is the same as dividing by zero. If you mod with zero, you'll generate a runtime error or exception. Check for this case rather than blowing up.

As discussed in Technique 20, make sure that the divide-by-zero isn't really caused by a design problem.

Technique 22: Write the Loop Increment/Decrement First

Category: Avoid crashes and unexpected results

Before

```
while(pdw < pdwMac)
    {
        dwCarry =
            (pdw+1 == pdwMac) ?
            dwCarry = 0 : dwCarry = *(pdw + 1)<<cBitsRight;
```

```
        *pdw >>= cBits;
        *pdw |= dwCarry;
    }
```

After

```
while(pdw < pdwMac)
    {
        dwCarry =
            (pdw+1 == pdwMac) ?
            dwCarry = 0 : dwCarry = *(pdw + 1)<<cBitsRight;
        *pdw >>= cBits;
        *pdw |= dwCarry;
        ++pdw;
    }
```

Whenever you write a loop, be sure to take care of the increment or decrement of the loop conditional before you write the rest of the code inside the loop. It is easy to get caught up in the excitement and challenge of writing the code for the inner body of the loop. Then, having finished that task, you forget to deal with the loop counter. As a result, you will most likely go into an infinite loop or else loop the wrong way.

See example: `BF::ShiftLeftBits()` in bits.cpp

Technique 23: `0 == a` versus `a == 0`

Category: Avoid stupid mistakes

Before

```
if (a == 0)
    cout << "It is 0";
```

After

```
if (0 == a)
    cout << "It is 0";
```

Many programmers, especially those moving from a language such as Basic, are used to = being used for assignment as well as for equality comparison. One way to avoid making this mistake is to place literals on the left when writing comparisons.

If you accidentally leave out one of the = signs in the "Before" code, a will be assigned the value 0 and the `if` will always evaluate false. If you accidentally leave out an = sign in the "After" code, the compiler will generate a syntax error.

Of course, using this technique is no substitute for single-stepping over every line of code that you write. Make sure that the code is doing what you expect it to be doing. Even look at the code generated by the compiler. You may find a difference between what you think you told the machine to do and what you actually told the machine to do (and in some rare cases, what the machine decided to do anyway).

Caveat

This only works when comparing variables to literals. It is a less intuitive way to write code, so it could end up driving you nuts. The better thing to do is to make sure you use = when you want to set a value and == when you want to compare a value.

Technique 24: Use Header Sentinels

Category: Compile your code

Before

```
const int clMax=256;
```

After

```
#ifndef _ALGOR_H
#define _ALGOR_H
const int clMax=256;
```

In order to organize code, one often includes .h files from other .h files. For example, `foo.c` might need `foo.h`; `foo.h` might include `globals.h`; `bar.c` might include `bar.h`, which also includes `globals.h`; and `baz.cpp` might need `foo.h` and `bar.h`. As a result, `baz.cpp` ends up including `globals.h` twice. Compilers don't like for you to define constants, classes, and structures more than once. In fact, they will complain quite loudly.

To avoid this problem, wrap your header files with sentinels. This is a fancy word for combining a #ifndef with a #define, as shown in the "After" code in this section. If the header file has already been loaded, then _ALGOR_H will be defined; the #ifndef will fail, and the stuff in the header file will be skipped. If _ALGOR_H wasn't already defined, then the header file has yet to be processed; everything inside the #ifndef will be processed.

Another option is to use #pragma once, if your compiler supports it. This pragma allows you to only include that header file once *and only once.* In theory, at least, it allows faster compiles since the compiler doesn't have to parse #ifdef sentinels at all.

See example: algor.h

Technique 25: Intrinsics Use Byte Counts

Category: Avoid crashes and unexpected results

Before

```
float *pfltBuf;
pfltBuf = (float *) GlobalAlloc(GMEM_FIXED, 4);
if (pfltBuf)
   memcpy(pfltBuf, pfltSrc, 4);
```

After

```
float *pfltBuf;
pfltBuf = (float *) GlobalAlloc(GMEM_FIXED, 4*sizeof(float));
if (pfltBuf)
   memcpy(pfltBuf, pfltSrc, 4*sizeof(float));
```

Length arguments to intrinsic functions are always measured in bytes. Make sure that you adjust the length according to the size of the structures you are manipulating. For example, if you are creating an array of floats, multiply the count by the size of a float. Do likewise for any custom structs.

Note that this is different than code that manipulates arrays or pointers, where the compiler automatically adjusts array dereferences and pointer arithmetic operations (increments, decrements, etc.) based on the structure size.

Technique 26: memcpy Uses Byte Counts

Category: Avoid crashes and unexpected results

Before

```
float pfltBuf[50];
memcpy(pfltBuf, pfltSrc, 4);
```

After

```
float pfltBuf[50];
memcpy(pfltBuf, pfltSrc, 4*sizeof(float));
```

We admit it. This is just a repeat of Technique 25. But it is important enough to repeat. When you use memcpy, you specify how much memory to copy in bytes. So if you want to copy four elements from an array, as is done in this example, make sure that you multiply the byte count by the size of the elements in the array. Otherwise, you'll just end up copying four bytes.

Technique 27: Use const instead of Numeric Literals

Category: Write maintainable code; avoid stupid mistakes

Before

```
for (int k = 0; k < 3; k++)
    {
    //First loop
    }

for (k = 0; k < 4; k++)
    {
    //Second loop. Woops. Wrong number of iterations
    }
```

After

```
const int NUMITEMS = 3;

for (int k = 0; k < NUMITEMS; k++)
```

```
    {
    //First loop
    }

for (k = 0; k < NUMITEMS; k++)
    {
    //Second loop
    }
```

There are many reasons to use constants instead of literals. First, they improve code readability. It is much easier to understand that the sample loop shown iterates over the number of items than it is to understand what some random value means. This is also true when defining constants for switch statements or return values. E_SITENOTFOUND is a lot easier to understand than 0x80001292.

Furthermore, by using constants, you can change the value once and have the change take place everywhere. For example, in the above fragment, by changing NUMITEMS to 4, all of the loops that iterate over the items will automatically update their loop counts. Unlike #define, constants declared with const have type established. This means that the compiler will use its normal type checking to make sure that you haven't used a constant in an inappropriate fashion.

Also, unlike macros, const values are visible within the debugger, making them useful for debugging.

See example: tips.h

Technique 28: const Precomputes Sizes

Category: Write cleaner code

Before

```
cdw = (cbitNeeded + sizeof(DWORD) * 8 - 1)/ (sizeof(DWORD) * 8);
```

After

```
const int cbitDWORD  = sizeof(DWORD) * 8;
cdw = (cbitNeeded + cbitDWORD - 1)/ cbitDWORD;
```

Anytime you use a constant, the compiler precomputes its value. This means there is no runtime cost for calculating the value.

Caveat

The compiler always precalculates constant portions of expressions, and when optimizations are turned on, it will even precalculate expressions that it determines won't change. So don't use this technique for getting performance gains; use it to make your code easier to read and maintain.

See example: bits.cpp

Technique 29: Sometimes You Need to Use #define instead of const

Category: Write maintainable code

Before

```
virtual BOOL FOpen(const char *szText) =0;
```

After

```
#define PURE =0;
virtual BOOL FOpen(const char *szText) PURE;
```

There are cases where you can't use const. Unlike const, #define provides string substitution. Because the strings are substituted during the code preprocessing stage, #define can thus be used for broader circumstances, such as creating macros. You also need to use #define for making declarations easier to understand. In the example shown here, we have created a pure function. It is a lot easier to understand this when looking at the "After" example.

See example: tips.h

Technique 30: Using an Assert instead of, or in addition to, Commenting Code

Category: Avoid crashes and unexpected results

Before

```
while(m_rgl[++i] < lKey);
        // There is no way i can go past the right
        // bound because lKey is picked up to be the
        // right most entry.
```

```
      do
      {
         j--;
         if(j < 0)
         {
```

After

```
while(m_rgl[++i] < lKey);
         // There is no way i can go past the right
         //bound because lKey is picked up to be the
         //right most entry.
         assert(i < m_clMac);

         do
         {
            j--;
            if(j < 0)
            {
```

Although it is very important to add comments about boundary expectations and other assumptions, you should also add asserts to make sure that those boundary conditions actually hold because sometimes what happens in code isn't what you expect, especially under stress conditions. That is, after all, the definition of a bug: The code isn't doing what you expect it to do (see Technique 144). Furthermore, a comment could become out of date. For example, perhaps you have a comment that states, "There is no way this value will be too large." Well, that may have been true when you started writing the program, but some change somewhere could invalidate that comment. The assert, however, will always be active. So if you assert when the value is too large, the assert will occur whenever the value is too large, no matter how you change your code.

Note also that asserts only work during debug builds. As a result, you get all the benefits of the assert when you are testing, but there is no performance or size impact when you create the retail version of the program.

See example: SArray::QuickSort() in bsrch.cpp

Technique 31: Handle the Exception Even If You Assert

Category: Avoid crashes

Before

```
assert(i < m_clMac);
//process stuff
```

After

```
assert(i < m_clMac);
if (i < m_clMac)
{
    //process stuff
```

Asserts are wonderful. They clearly tell you something has gone wrong. Or rather, if you are running a debug build, asserts will fire when something goes wrong. So always put asserts in your code. You can't rely on them for preventing problems, however, because they aren't in retail builds. Always handle the error condition in addition to asserting, so that if you have a problem at runtime you won't crash or otherwise puke.

See example: SArray::QuickSort() in bsrch.cpp

Technique 32: Carefully Choose Signed or Unsigned Types

Category: Avoid unexpected results

Before

```
int nVal;
nVal >> 4;
```

After

```
unsigned int nVal;
nVal >> 4;
```

The compiler will automatically supply sign correction code when manipulating signed numbers. For example, shifting right a signed number 0x80000000 results in 0xC0000000 instead of the expected 0x40000000. This is because the compiler recognizes that the number is signed and does an SAR instruction, not an SHR. In other words, it treats 0x80000000 as a negative number and ensures that the resulting shifted value is also negative.

If, on the other hand, you shift right an unsigned value (such as an unsigned int or a DWORD), the compiler won't preserve the sign bit and you will get the value you expect.

See example: bits.cpp

Technique 33: Be Careful When You Mix Signed and Unsigned Values

Category: Avoid stupid mistakes

Before

```
unsigned int nNewSamples;
int nBufSize;

nNewSamples = -1;
nBufSize = 10;

cout << "Starting" << endl;

while (nNewSamples >= nBufSize)
{
   cout << "Loop" << endl;
   nNewSamples = 0;
}
```

After

```
int nNewSamples;
int nBufSize;

nNewSamples = -1;
nBufSize = 10;

cout << "Starting" << endl;

while (nNewSamples >= nBufSize)
{
   cout << "Loop" << endl;
   nNewSamples = 0;
}
```

Signed and unsigned numbers have different ranges but can be cast from one to the other. This means that you may accidentally compare one to the other and get unexpected results if the size of the unsigned number is large enough to be treated as a negative number when it is cast to a signed number (or vice versa). As a result, you could end up with a loop that never ends or all types of other interesting side effects.

For example, consider the "Before" code for this technique, where we are comparing the value of an unsigned to a signed value. The unsigned value is set to -1. Because it is unsigned, it gets turned into a very large number. The loop compares that number to 10 and comes up with true and the loop thus executes.

By contrast, in the "After" code, both numbers are signed and the comparison is false.

Of course, the sample shown for this technique is rather simplistic, and it is easy to see how the problem occurs. Real-life code will make finding the problem harder. In general, don't mix signed and unsigned numbers. If you do, be careful.

Technique 34: Use Parentheses If You Need Them

Category: Avoid stupid mistakes

Before

```
if(!(i+1 % 64))
    cout << "\n";
```

After

```
if(!((i+1) % 64))
    cout << "\n";
```

If you are not positive about what operations have precedence, use parentheses to make expressions clearer. For example, % has higher precedence than +. Thus, the expression in the "Before" code is equivalent to the following:

```
if(!(i + (1 % 64))
    cout << "\n";
```

This is certainly not the desired code.

See example: `BF::PrintBits()` in bits.cpp

Technique 35: Use Parentheses If You Need Them

Category: Avoid stupid mistakes

Before

```
#define FOO j + 1
x = k * FOO;
```

After

```
#define FOO (j + 1)
x = k * FOO;
```

Be especially wary of parentheses when using #define to create expressions. In particular, make sure that you have enough of them. It's okay to err on the side of adding too many.

Code may look perfectly correct in the #define, but order of operations can cause bugs when you use the defined value in an expression. For example, the "Before" and "After" codes for this technique will create very different results.

When in doubt, add parentheses.

Technique 36: Always Treat Warnings as Errors

Category: Avoid stupid mistakes; write maintainable code

Before

```
unsigned int nNewSamples;
int nBufSize;

nNewSamples = -1;
nBufSize = 10;

cout << "Starting" << endl;

while (nNewSamples >= nBufSize)
{
    cout << "Loop" << endl;
    nNewSamples = 0;
}
```

After

```
int nNewSamples;
int nBufSize;

nNewSamples = -1;
nBufSize = 10;

cout << "Starting" << endl;
```

```
while (nNewSamples >= nBufSize)
{
   cout << "Loop" << endl;
   nNewSamples = 0;
}
```

Warnings hide potential errors that are always worth examining. Sure, you're busy compiling, and you know it's just some silly message about casting between a double and a float. Big deal. Well, it very well could be a big deal. You're always better off fixing the issue. This is especially important when working on large projects or with other people. If you don't fix the trivial warnings, important ones could get lost in the sea of trivial ones. In turn, you may not know which warnings are critical when looking at someone else's code. Also, it's just plain sloppy.

For example, the "Before" code in this example compares a signed integer with an unsigned integer. The compiler generates a warning. If you don't fix it, the code won't work the way you expect.

Use the compiler to treat warnings as errors. From the command line, use the /WX flag. Or, from the environment, do the following:

1. Select Project→Settings.

2. Click on the C/C++ tab.

3. Select the General category.

4. Click on the Warnings as Errors checkbox.

Technique 37: Always Use at Least Warning Level 3

Category: Avoid stupid mistakes

It takes a lot less time to fix a warning than it does to debug code. Let the compiler do as much of the dirty work for you as possible. Warning messages that seem trivial may really be pointing out nasty potential problems. We suggest using warning level 3.

From the command line, use the /W3 or /W4 flag. Or, from the environment do the following:

1. Select Project→Settings.

2. Click on the C/C++ tab.

3. Select the General category.

4. Select Level 3 or Level 4 from the Warning Level drop down.

Technique 38: Be Careful When Using \ in Strings

Category: Avoid unexpected results

Before

```
Literal li("this\sis\sa\stest1");
```

After

```
Literal li("this\\sis\\sa\\stest1");
```

Remember that \ is an escape character. If you really want to have a \ appear inside of a string (for example, for a regular expression match or for a directory path), be sure to use \\ instead.

See example: TestRegExp() in regexp.cpp

Technique 39: Be Careful When You Mix C and C++

Category: Compile your code

Before

```
const int NULL=0;
```

After

```
//Nothing . . .
```

The "Before" code looks darn innocuous, doesn't it? What could be simpler? Well, when we compiled this code we got the following error messages:

```
C:\book\exp\drg.h(7) : error C2143: syntax error : missing ';' before 'constant'
C:\book\exp\drg.h(7) : fatal error C1004: unexpected end of file found
```

What the heck does that mean? This problem illustrates one of the many things that can go wrong when you mix C and C++. In this example, one of the C runtime header files defined NULL:

```
#define NULL 0
```

Our friendly C++ line was thus converted to the following:

```
const int 0=0;
```

This in turn led to the confusing error message.

Technique 40: Determining If a Constant Is Already Defined

Category: Compile your code

Before

```
#define NULL 0
```

After

```
#ifdef NULL
#pragma message("NULL already defined")
#else
#define NULL 0
#endif
```

You can avoid error messages (including the confusing one discussed in Technique 39) if you check whether a constant is defined before you define it. Because this check is done during preprocessing, it has no impact on performance.

See example: drg.h

Technique 41: Know Exactly What Functions Do (At Least If You Use Them)

Category: Avoid crashes and unexpected results

Before

```
const Literal &operator=(const char *pch)
{
    strncpy(m_rgch, pch, sizeof(m_rgch)-1);
```

```
    return *this;
}
```

After

```
const Literal &operator=(const char *pch)
{
    strncpy(m_rgch, pch, sizeof(m_rgch)-2);
    m_rgch[sizeof(m_rgch) - 1] = 0;
    return *this;
}
```

You need to understand exactly how functions behave to make sure that you don't accidentally interject errors and edge cases. In this example, we are copying from a char * into our class. The string in our class has a fixed size, whereas the char * could point to a string of any length. So we use the strncpy function rather than strcpy to make sure that we don't copy more than what is available in our buffer.

Seems simple, yes? Well, let's take a look at the documentation of strncpy from the Visual C++ product manual:

> The strncpy function copies the initial count characters of strSource to strDest and returns strDest. If count is less than or equal to the length of strSource, a null character is NOT appended automatically to the copied string. If count is greater than the length of strSource, the destination string is padded with null characters up to length count.

This means that we need to consider two cases: (1) what happens when the string we're copying is smaller than the buffer and (2) what happens when the string is the same size or larger than the buffer.

If the string is smaller, we're in good shape. A nice null-terminated string will be copied into our buffer. If the string is larger or the same size as the buffer, then what gets copied will not be null terminated. That could lead to all types of problems. (For example, if you call strlen on a string that is not null terminated, you could wait a very long time as the runtime searches throughout all of memory, only stopping if it finds a zero.)

Because we need to account for this case, we always leave room at the end of the buffer for a null character. That's why we subtract two from the size of the buffer. We then make sure that the last character in the buffer is always zero.

See example: Literal::&operator= in regexp.h

Technique 42: Make Sure Strings Are Null Terminated

Category: Avoid crashes and unexpected results

Before

```
const Literal &operator=(const char *pch)
{
    strncpy(m_rgch, pch, sizeof(m_rgch)-1);
    return *this;
}
```

After

```
const Literal &operator=(const char *pch)
{
    strncpy(m_rgch, pch, sizeof(m_rgch)-2);
    m_rgch[sizeof(m_rgch) - 1] = 0;
    return *this;
}
```

All string functions expect strings to be null terminated. This becomes an issue whenever you use commands such as memcpy to copy substrings. If you forget to make sure there is a null at the end of the strings, pandemonium can break loose when you perform string operations. You can easily cause infinite loops, trash memory, and so forth.

See example: Literal::&operator= in regexp.h

Technique 43: Check the Actual Size

Category: Avoid crashes and unexpected results

Before

```
//The buffer size
const cchLiteral = 256;
private:
    char m_rgch[cchLiteral-10];

public:
const Literal &operator=(const char *pch)
```

```
{
    strncpy(m_rgch, pch, cchLiteral-1);
    return *this;
}
```

After

```
//The buffer size
const cchLiteral = 256;
private:
    char m_rgch[cchLiteral-10];

const Literal &operator=(const char *pch)
{
    strncpy(m_rgch, pch, sizeof(m_rgch)-2);
    return *this;
}
```

Okay, maybe this code is slightly contrived. You'd never do anything like this, right? A constant is created indicating the desired size of a buffer. In the "Before" code, we believe the comment when it says that the constant indicates the buffer size. But as you can see in the code, the programmer may have actually done something completely different. If you merely trusted the comment and based your copy on the constant, you'd crash. A much safer practice is to check the actual size of the object using `sizeof`. Because this is done at compilation, there isn't any performance penalty.

See example: `Literal::&operator=` in regexp.h

Technique 44: Use Inline Functions instead of Macros

Category: Avoid stupid mistakes

Before

```
#define OutputIMacro(i) (cout << i << '\n')
void TestInLine()
{
    OutputIMacro(11);
    OutputIMacro("Test1");
}
```

After

```
class InLineTest
{
public:
    void OutputI(int i)
    {
        cout << i << '\n';
    }
};

void TestInLine()
{
    InLineTest ilt;

    ilt.OutputI(10);
    // this generates compile error - C:\book\misc\misc.cpp(126) : error C2664:
    // 'OutputI' : cannot convert parameter 1 from 'char [5]' to 'int'
    //ilt.OutputI("Test");
}
```

Macros are useful, but they provide no type checking. For example, suppose we want a routine that prints out the value of an integer. We could use a macro, as shown in the "Before" code for this technique. Note, however, that the macro very happily processes any argument passed to it. You can use it with an integer as desired. But, you can also pass in a string or anything else too.

By contrast, the "After" code uses an inline method. Because it is a method, the compiler performs type checking. Thus, if we uncommented out the line that attempts to output a string, we'd get a syntax error.

See example: TestInLine() in misc.cpp

CHAPTER 3

Dealing with Compiler-Generated Code

YOU WRITE CODE IN C++. THE COMPILER WRITES CODE in Assembly. Guess which one the user receives? If you understand what type of code the compiler generates, you can learn how to write more efficient code. In this chapter, we examine a few techniques you can employ to make your code more efficient.

Technique 45: Constructors and Destructors Are Automatically Created for You

Category: Write faster code

Source

```cpp
class base1
{
private:
   char sz[256];
   int i;
   float f;
public:
   base1(base1 &b1)
   {
      cout << "base1 copy ctor\n";
   }
   base1()
   {
      cout << "base1 constructor\n";
   }
   ~base1()
   {
      cout << "base1 destructor\n";
```

```
    }
};

class Derived1 : public base1
{
public:
    Derived1(Derived1 &derived1) : base1(derived1)
    {
        cout << "Derived1 copy ctor\n";
    }
    Derived1()
    {
        cout << "Derived1 constructor\n";
    }
    ~Derived1()
    {
        cout << "Derived1 destructor\n";
    }
};
void TestVirtualDTor()
{
    pd11 = new Derived1;
}
```

Assembly for Boldfaced Line

```
00413566 push   108h
0041356B call   operator new(0x00404830)
00413570 add    esp,4
00413573 mov    dword ptr [ebp-164h],eax
00413579 mov    dword ptr [ebp-4],5
00413580 cmp    dword ptr [ebp-164h],0
00413587 je     TestVirtualDTor(0x004135a3)+2BFh
00413589 mov    eax,dword ptr [pd11]
0041358F push   eax
00413590 mov    ecx,dword ptr [ebp-164h]
00413596 call   @ILT+25(??0Derived1@@QAE@AAV0@@Z)(0x00401019)
0041359B mov    dword ptr [ebp-188h],eax
004135A1 jmp    TestVirtualDTor(0x004135ad)+2C9h
004135A3 mov    dword ptr [ebp-188h],0
```

```
004135AD mov    ecx,dword ptr [ebp-188h]
004135B3 mov    dword ptr [ebp-168h],ecx
004135B9 mov    dword ptr [ebp-4],0FFFFFFFFh
004135C0 mov    edx,dword ptr [ebp-168h]
004135C6 mov    dword ptr [pd12],edx
```

The single new looks fairly innocent. But you will note that a lot of code is generated and called. Even if you omit constructors and destructors for the class, they are automatically generated.

See example: `TestVirtualDTor()` in inherit.cpp

Technique 46: Wrap new to Save Space

Category: Write faster code

Before

```
pref = new RefCounted();
```

Assembly for Boldfaced Line

```
0040E51B push   4
0040E51D call   operator new(0x00403430)
0040E522 add    esp,4
0040E525 mov    dword ptr [ebp-14h],eax
0040E528 mov    dword ptr [ebp-4],0
0040E52F cmp    dword ptr [ebp-14h],0
0040E533 je     TestRefCounted(0x0040e542)+42h
0040E535 mov    ecx,dword ptr [ebp-14h]
0040E538 call   @ILT+40(?newRefCounted@RefCounted@@SAPAV1@XZ)(0x00401028)
0040E53D mov    dword ptr [ebp-1Ch],eax
0040E540 jmp    TestRefCounted(0x0040e549)+49h
0040E542 mov    dword ptr [ebp-1Ch],0
0040E549 mov    eax,dword ptr [ebp-1Ch]
0040E54C mov    dword ptr [ebp-18h],eax
0040E54F mov    dword ptr [ebp-4],0FFFFFFFFh
0040E556 mov    ecx,dword ptr [ebp-18h]
0040E559 mov    dword ptr [pref],ecx
```

After

```
class RefCounted
{
public:
    static RefCounted *newRefCounted()
    {
        return new RefCounted;
    }
};

pref = RefCounted::newRefCounted();
```

The new operator generates a lot of inline code. It calls the new operator and then calls the constructor, as you can see in the assembly listing shown here. Every time you call new, you get this wad of generated code.

In modern processors, you pay a bigger performance hit for having verbose code than for having an extra function call because larger code can cause second-ary cache hits. (Or in a worse situation, it can force the processor to bring in code that is not in a cache.) The cache swapping takes more time than does an extra function call.

With the "After" code for this technique, we've created a member function that does the new. We call that member function rather than calling new ourselves. As a result, there is far less generated code and the performance should increase.

See example: class RefCounted in access.cpp

Technique 47: If You Overload new, Overload delete

Category: Avoid crashes and memory leaks

Before

```
void *operator new(size_t cbAlloc)
{
    return malloc(cbAlloc);
}
```

After

```
void *operator new(size_t cbAlloc)
{
    return malloc(cbAlloc);
}
void operator delete(void * pv)
{
    free(pv);
}
```

You need to use the same memory manager to deallocate memory as you use to allocate memory. Otherwise, you will crash when the deallocator (i.e., the wrong deallocator) tries to free up memory that it doesn't know anything about. For example, if you use the Windows heap manager to allocate memory, use HeapFree to clean up the memory instead of the default delete.

See example: class RefCounted in access.cpp

Technique 48: The + Operator Generates Considerable Overhead

Category: Write cleaner code

Source

```
String operator+(const String&string) const
    {
        String stringNew(m_pch);

        stringNew.Append(string.m_pch, string.m_cch);
        return stringNew;
    }
```

When you create a + operator, a lot of things happen. In the example shown here, a new string class is constructed. The two strings are concatenated into this new string. Then, the compiler automatically instantiates a String variable on the stack frame of the caller. This is for the return value. Its copy constructor is called with stringNew as a parameter, which copies the contents to the return variable. Then, before the function exits, stringNew is destroyed.

If we had just concatenated the strings directly with Append, we could have done so more efficiently. Instead, the operator resulted in two instances of temporary string variables, and it called the copy constructor.

Here's the code that gets generated for the operator:

```
00401791 lea    eax,dword ptr [stringNew]
00401794 push   eax
00401795 mov    ecx,dword ptr [__$ReturnUdt]  ;The string variable where the actual
                concatenated string is returned
00401798 call   @ILT+75(??0String@@QAE@ABVO@@Z)(0x0040104b) ;copy ctor on this
                string with stringNew as parameter
0040179D mov    ecx,dword ptr [ebp-1Ch]
004017A0 or     ecx,1
004017A3 mov    dword ptr [ebp-1Ch],ecx
004017A6 mov    byte ptr [ebp-4],0
004017AA lea    ecx,dword ptr [stringNew]
004017AD call   @ILT+15(??1String@@QAE@XZ)(0x0040100f) ;dtor for stringNew because
                it's an automatic variable
004017B2 mov    eax,dword ptr [__$ReturnUdt]
145:   }
004017B5 mov    ecx,dword ptr [ebp-0Ch]
004017B8 mov    dword ptr fs:[0],ecx
004017BF mov    esp,ebp
004017C1 pop    ebp
004017C2 ret    8
```

CHAPTER 4

Pointers and Memory

THIS CHAPTER DISCUSSES TECHNIQUES THAT CAN help you write safer, more efficient code when working with pointers and memory. Some of these techniques, such as not freeing memory multiple times, are just common sense. Others, such as using smart pointers, are slightly more sophisticated.

Technique 49: Check for Successful Allocation

Category: Avoid crashes

Before

```
pdw = new DWORD[cdw];
memset(pdw, OL, sizeof(DWORD) * cdw);
```

After

```
pdw = new DWORD[cdw];
if(pdw)
   memset(pdw, OL, sizeof(DWORD) * cdw);
```

Yeah, we know, we've talked about this one before in Technique 19. But checking return codes is particularly important when allocating memory. If you allocate memory, make sure the allocation has succeeded before you use the memory.

See example: class BF:FSetSize() in bits.cpp

Technique 50: Free Once, Not Often

Category: Avoid crashes

Before

```
LEX::~LEX()
{
    delete m_pstream;
}
```

After

```
LEX::~LEX()
{
    if(m_pstream)
        delete m_pstream;
}
```

Always be sure memory exists before freeing it. Otherwise, you'll get the big kaboom. For example, you may have freed the memory already. Or perhaps, due to some problem, it wasn't allocated in the first place.

If you free in places other than the destructor, be sure to set the member pointer variables to null in order to avoid freeing them more than once:

```
if (m_pstream)
{
    delete m_pstream;
    m_pstream = NULL;
}
```

Technique 51: Make Sure You Can Allocate before You Replace

Category: Avoid crashes

Before

```
pdw = new DWORD[cdw];
if(m_rgdw)
```

```
       delete [] m_rgdw;
m_rgdw = pdw;
```

After

```
pdw = new DWORD[cdw];
if(pdw)
{
    if(m_rgdw)
        delete [] m_rgdw;
    m_rgdw = pdw;
```

The code listed for this technique is an excerpt from a routine that replaces a memory buffer with a buffer of a different size. In the "Before" code, we simply deleted the old buffer and swapped in the new. Instead, you should make sure that the new allocation works before deleting the old.

If the memory allocation fails, you are most likely in a low-memory condition. This often spells trouble. One approach is to assert so that you can see that you are out of memory. However, in low-memory conditions, you may not have enough resources to put up the message box showing the assert. Instead, consider using trace calls.

Caveat

You can of course set the buffer pointer to null if the new allocation failed, if you want. In that case, however, all subsequent operations that manipulate the buffer need to check whether a buffer exists.

See example: BF::FSetSize() in bits.cpp

Technique 52: Be Prepared for Multiple Calls to Buffer Allocation Methods

Category: Avoid memory leaks

Before

```
pdw = new DWORD[cdw];
if(pdw)
{
    m_rgdw = pdw;
```

After

```
pdw = new DWORD[cdw];
if(pdw)
{
    if(m_rgdw)
        delete [] m_rgdw;
    m_rgdw = pdw;
```

If you have code that allocates a buffer based on a call outside of the constructor, be prepared for the routine to be called more than once. For example, the code shown for this technique is an excerpt from a method that sets the size of a memory buffer. The method can be called any number of times. Thus, within the routine, we allocate a buffer for the new size. If that is successful, we delete the old buffer and then set the buffer pointer to point to the newly allocated buffer.

Note that we don't delete the old buffer in the "Before" code. Thus, every time the method is called, we leak memory.

See example: BF::FSetSize() in bits.cpp

Technique 53: Don't Return Pointers to Automatic Variables

Category: Avoid crashes and unexpected results

Before

```
char * strdup2(char *szSrc)
{
    char szDst[256];

    if(strlen(szSrc)>sizeof(szDst)-1)
        return NULL;
    lstrcpy(szDst, szSrc);
    return szDst;
}
```

After

```
char * strdup2(char *szSrc)
{
    char *szDst;
```

```
    szDst = new char [lstrlen(szSrc)+1];
    if(szDst == NULL)
        return NULL;
    lstrcpy(szDst, szSrc);
    return szDst;
}
```

Automatic variables (those that are allocated off of the stack, such as local variables) are transient. They last as long as a function has scope. After you return from a function, the variables are automatically destroyed.

Let's take a look at the "Before" code for this technique. We first allocate a buffer on the stack, called szDest. We then copy a string into the buffer and return a pointer to the buffer. Looks simple enough, yes? Well, as soon as strdup2 ends, the stack gets cleaned up. Thus, szDest is now invalid and can get overwritten at any time. Yet that is what we just returned a pointer to. As a result, the pointer points to junk.

The "After" code addresses this issue by allocating memory off of the heap and returning a pointer to that memory. Heap memory is not reclaimed when a function ends. Thus, the "After" code is safe.

For another approach, the calling routine could allocate memory and pass the pointer to the buffer to fill to strdup2. You'll see that approach used by many of the Win32 APIs.

Technique 54: Always Initialize to a Known State

Category: Avoid crashes and unexpected results

Before

```
BOOL  BF::FSetSize(DWORD cbitNeeded)
{
    DWORD *pdw;
    long cdw;

    cdw = (cbitNeeded + cbitDWORD - 1)/ cbitDWORD;
    pdw = new DWORD[cdw];
    if(pdw)
    {
        if(m_rgdw)
            delete [] m_rgdw;
```

After

```
BOOL  BF::FSetSize(DWORD cbitNeeded)
{
    DWORD *pdw;
    long cdw;

    cdw = (cbitNeeded + cbitDWORD - 1)/ cbitDWORD;
    pdw = new DWORD[cdw];
    if(pdw)
    {
        if(m_rgdw)
            delete [] m_rgdw;
        memset(pdw, 0L, sizeof(DWORD) * cdw);
```

It is easy to assume that a variable or array will, by default, have the value that you hope it has. Unfortunately, assumptions and hope don't get you too far when programming. Therefore, always initialize variables and arrays before they get used.

The example shown for this technique is straightforward because the memory is allocated in the procedure where it is used. In other cases, you may have a buffer that is globally allocated. Make sure it is properly initialized before it gets used. I fondly remember some code I wrote for manipulating wave forms. I created a global buffer for averaging in results of transformations using a noise-reduction technique called overlap and add. It worked great—except for the first time through, where I didn't initialize the buffer and thus got a very surprising, noisy result.

See example: BF::FSetSize() in bits.cpp

Technique 55: Avoid Self-Referential Copies

Category: Write faster code; avoid unexpected results

Before

```
void Drgbase::Copy(const Drgbase &drgbase)
{
    m_rgb = (BYTE *)malloc(LCB);
    if(m_rgb)
    {
        memcpy(m_rgb, drgbase.m_rgb, LCB);
    }
}
```

After

```
void Drgbase::Copy(const Drgbase &drgbase)
{
    if(&drgbase == this)
        return;

    m_rgb = (BYTE *)malloc(LCB);
    if(m_rgb)
    {
        memcpy(m_rgb, drgbase.m_rgb, LCB);
    }
}
```

Why waste time copying memory when you don't need to? Furthermore, as we show in Technique 78, sometimes side effects of self-referential copies can be even more dangerous, causing data loss or crashes.

See example: Drgbase::Copy() in drg.cpp

Technique 56: Use const *

Category: Avoid unexpected results

Before

```
void String::InitString(char * pch, int cch)
{
    m_cch = 0;
    m_pch = NULL;
    if(cch)
```

After

```
void String::InitString(const char * pch, int cch)
{
    m_cch = 0;
    m_pch = NULL;
    if(cch)
```

Putting a const in front of a pointer guarantees that the contents in the buffer will not change. For example, in the "Before" code for this technique, the InitString method could change the contents of the initializing string if it wanted to. In the

"After" example, the `InitString` method cannot change the contents of the initializing string. This provides an extra level of safety that can prevent unexpected memory overwrites.

See example: `String::InitString()` in string.cpp

Technique 57: Avoiding Errors When Using const const

Category: Compile your code

Source

```
void TestConstConst1(char const * const*ppch)
{
    char ch;
    *ppch = &ch; //Error
    **ppch = ch; //Error
}
void TestConstConst2(char *const*ppch)
{
    char ch;
    *ppch = &ch; //Error
    **ppch = ch;
}
void TestConstConst3( char const**ppch)
{
    char ch;
    *ppch = &ch;
    **ppch = ch; //Error
}
```

Remember that const applies from left to right. In `TestConstConst1`, the left const applies to the char `*`. The right const applies to the char `**`. Thus, in `TestConstConst1`, neither the pointer nor the characters pointed to can change. Both assignments in the body of the code will generate errors.

In `TestConstConst2`, char `*` is a const. Therefore, the contents pointed to can't change. But the pointer to the contents can change. So the first assignment generates an error, but the second does not.

In `TestConstConst3`, the char `**` is a const. Thus, the contents pointed to can change, but the pointer itself can't. Therefore, the first assignment is okay, but the second assignment causes a syntax error.

See example: TestConstConst1(), TestConstConst2(), and TestConstConst3() in misc.cpp

Technique 58: Use Smart Pointers

Category: Avoid memory leaks

Source

```
template <class T> class BaseSmartPointer
{
private:
    BaseSmartPointer<T>&operator=(BaseSmartPointer<T>&bsp)
    {
        return *this;
    }
protected:
    T *m_pt;
public:
    BaseSmartPointer(T *pt=NULL) : m_pt(pt)
    {
    }
    virtual ~BaseSmartPointer()
    {
        if(m_pt)
            delete m_pt;
        m_pt = NULL;
    }

    T &operator*() const
    {
        return *m_pt;
    }

    T*operator=(T *pt)
    {
        m_pt = pt;
        return m_pt;
    }
};
```

Smart pointers automatically free the memory associated with a pointer when that pointer is deleted, helping to prevent a common source of memory leaks. Creating a smart pointer is easy: You replace the intrinsic pointer type with a templatized class. Now, you might think that this is a waste of space. It turns out, however, that there isn't that much additional overhead, and the benefit is usually worth it.

For even stronger leak prevention, combine smart pointers with reference counting.

See example: BaseSmartPointer in smartptr.h

Technique 59: Use Smart Pointers for Objects

Category: Avoid memory leaks

Source

```
template <class T> class ObjectSmartPointer : public BaseSmartPointer <T>
{
public:
    ObjectSmartPointer(T* pt=NULL) : BaseSmartPointer<T>(pt)
    {
    }


    T* operator=(T *pt)
    {
        return BaseSmartPointer<T>::operator=(pt);
    }

    T *operator->() const
    {
        return m_pt;
    }
};
```

Like smart pointers for intrinsics, smart pointers for objects automatically delete memory associated with a pointer when the pointer is destroyed. The class in this example is derived from the BaseSmartPointer class shown in the previous technique (Technique 58). The main difference is that the class shown here adds support for the -> operator. If you try to use it with an intrinsic type, such as an int, the compiler will give you a syntax error because the -> is not available. This error message for misuse provides yet another level of safety.

See example: ObjectSmartPointer in smartptr.h

Technique 60: Custom Memory Allocators and Smart Pointers

Category: Avoid crashes

The smart pointer classes shown in smartptr.h automatically delete the memory associated with a pointer when the smart pointer is destroyed. The classes do so by calling the delete command in the class destructor. This only works, however, when the memory associated with the pointer has been allocated with new. You need to make sure that the memory deletion command corresponds to the memory creation command. For example, if you allocated memory with HeapAlloc, you'd need to free it with HeapFree.

Technique 61: Don't Blow Your Buffers

Category: Avoid crashes and unexpected results

Before

```
const Literal &operator=(const char *pch)
{
    strcpy(m_rgch, pch);
    return *this;
}
```

After

```
const Literal &operator=(const char *pch)
{
    strncpy(m_rgch, pch, sizeof(m_rgch)-2);
    m_rgch[sizeof(m_rgch) - 1] = 0;
    return *this;
}
```

Unless your buffers have been visited by a marketing team, they are finite in length. Remember this anytime you do a copy. In other words, check the size of the buffer before doing your copy. This is particularly important to remember if you are using an intrinsic such as strcpy. In the example shown for this technique, we've switched from strcpy to strncpy to make sure that we don't copy off the end of the buffer.

Technique 62: Create a Memory Manager That Detects Leaks

Category: Avoid memory leaks

No matter how much you review your code, you are probably going to have a few bugs in it. One way to help prevent memory leaks is to create a custom memory allocator that detects leaks. When the process terminates and the memory allocator is destroyed, it can spit out warnings or asserts if memory has been allocated but not freed. You can use that information to track down how leaks have occurred.

Technique 63: Global versus Class-Specific Memory Allocators

Category: Write faster code

You can overload new globally or locally. If you overload new globally, you establish how memory will be allocated for your entire program. If you overload new within a class definition, you establish how memory will be allocated for a particular class. Overloading for a particular class lets you write a memory allocator optimized for the particular usage pattern of that class.

Caveat

The more memory allocators you create, the more memory allocator debugging you will need to do.

CHAPTER 5

Arrays

ARRAYS ARE A COMMONLY USED DATA STRUCTURE. They are easy to create and provide extremely fast retrieval times. In this chapter, you will learn some techniques to avoid problems and improve the way you use arrays.

Technique 64: Use delete [ ] with Arrays

Category: Avoid crashes

Before

```
pdw = new DWORD[cdw];
if (pdw)
    delete pdw;
```

After

```
pdw = new DWORD[cdw];
if (pdw)
    delete [] pdw;
```

If you allocate an array, you must delete an array. It's just that simple.
See example: BF::~BF() in bits.cpp

Technique 65: Avoid Index Underflow

Category: Avoid crashes and unexpected results

Before

```
do
{
    j--;
}
while(m_rgl[j] > lKey);
```

After

```
do
{
    j--;
    if(j < 0)
    {
        assert("j is < 0");
        break;
    }
}
while(m_rgl[j] > lKey);
```

Before you dereference an element in an array, make sure that the index is within the array bounds. Otherwise, you will reference memory outside of the array. You might crash. Or you might write over something you really didn't want to and then have one heck of a time trying to track down what went wrong. In the sample code for this technique, we make sure that the index does not go below zero.

See example: SArray::QuickSort() in bsrch.cp

Technique 66: Avoid Index Overflow

Category: Avoid crashes and unexpected results

Before

```
class Buf {
    private:
        const int bufsize = 200;
        int  buf[bufsize];

    public:
        int getVal(int nOffset)
        {
            return buf[nOffset];
        }
};
```

After

```
class Buf {
    private:
        const int bufsize = 200;
        int  buf[bufsize];

    public:
        int getVal(int nOffset)
        {
            if (nOffset < sizeof(buf) && nOffset > 0)
                return buf[nOffset];
            else
                return 0;
        }
};
```

As in the previous technique (Technique 65), before you dereference an element in an array, you need to make sure that the index is within the array bounds. If you don't, you will reference memory outside of the array and perhaps crash or write over something you really didn't want to and then be hard pressed to figure out what went wrong. In the sample code in this section, we again check that the index does not go outside of the array bounds.

Technique 67: foo[K] Is the Same as foo.operator[ ](K)

Category: Write cleaner code

Source

```
T&Peek(void)
    {
        return operator[](LcMac() - 1);
        //return *this[LcMac()-1];
    }
};
```

The following code:

```
foo[k]
```

is equivalent to this code:

```
foo.operator[](k)
```

The latter is usually a bit more complex looking. However, the latter syntax is nice when you need to perform array indexing on the `this` pointer, as you can see in the "Source" code for this technique.

If you don't like the operator notation, you can always use the array index notation instead, as is shown in the sample. In that case, be sure to note the pointer dereference.

Technique 68: An Array Is a Pointer

Category: Avoid crashes; compile your code

Source

```
void ProcC(char *pchBuf)
{
}
void ProcD()
{
    char *pch;
    char rgch[20];

    pch = rgch;
    pch = (char *)&rgch;

    ProcC(pch);
}
```

A pointer to an array is the array itself. Looking at the "Source" code shown for this technique, you can see that &rgch and rgch are one and the same. Note that, if you don't include the type cast, you'll get a syntax error.

CHAPTER 6

Classes

THIS AND THE NEXT FIVE CHAPTERS FOCUS ON TECHNIQUES relating to object-oriented programming. We'll begin with some general techniques designed to improve the way you use and program classes and then move on to some more advanced stuff.

Technique 69: Initialize Member Variables

Category: Avoid unexpected results

Before

```
class String {
private:
    const int m_cchTest;
    int m_cch;
    char *m_pch;
public:
    String(void)
    {
    }

    ~String(void)
    {
        if(m_pch)
            delete m_pch;
    }
};
```

After

```
class String {
private:
    const int m_cchTest;
    int m_cch;
    char *m_pch;
public:
    String(void) : m_cch(0), m_cchTest(10)
    {
        m_pch = NULL;
    }

    ~String(void)
    {
        if(m_pch)
            delete m_pch;
    }
};
```

Just as you must initialize local variables, you must initialize all of your member variables. In fact, it is even more important to initialize member variables because it can be harder to figure out what is going wrong when you don't, simply because the variables live across function boundaries. All sorts of bad things can happen if you don't initialize your variables. Most likely, calculations will be incorrect and you will possibly crash. For example, in the "Before" code for this technique, we don't initialize the memory pointer to NULL. If the destructor is called before the pointer is set to a valid value, the delete could be called on a random value. Memory allocators don't like freeing up pointers into outer space; they usually let you know by crashing.

Make it a habit to initialize member variables as soon as you define them. That will keep you out of trouble.

There are two ways to initialize member variables, as discussed in the next technique. Both approaches are used in the sample you just examined.

See example: class String in string.cpp

Technique 70: Use Initialization Lists

Category: Write faster code

Before

```
class String {
private:
   const int m_cchTest;
   int m_cch;
   char *m_pch;
public:
   String(void)
   {
      m_cch = 0;
      m_cchTest = 10;
   }
};
```

After

```
class String {
private:
   const int m_cchTest;
   int m_cch;
   char *m_pch;
public:
   String(void) : m_cch(0), m_cchTest(10), m_pch(NULL)
   {
   }
};
```

You can initialize variables either inside a constructor or by using an initialization list. It is more efficient to use an initialization list when initializing nonintrinsic types. When you initialize inside the constructor, the default initialization for the variables takes place and then the assignment occurs inside the constructor. When you initialize with the initialization list, the values provided are used during initialization and you thus avoid the double step of performing the assignment.

Initializations that require expressions—such as the code that follows—need to be done in the constructor:

```
m_cch = globalBitRate * 44000 / phaseOfMoon;
```

See example: class String in string.cpp

Technique 71: Don't Initialize consts inside the Body of the Constructor

Category: Compile your code

Before

```
class String {
private:
    const int m_cchTest;
public:
    String(void)
    {
        m_cchTest = 10;
    }
};
```

After

```
class String {
private:
    const int m_cchTest;
public:
    String(void) : m_cchTest(10)
    {
    }
};
```

By definition, const values can't change. You can initialize them in the initialization list but not inside the constructor.

See example: class String in string.cpp

Technique 72: const Member Variables Allocate Memory

Category: Write cleaner code

Source

```
static const long s_lStaticConst = 1001;
const long g_lNonStaticConst = 1000;
class CWithConst
{
private:
   int m_i;
   const int m_iConst;
};
class CWithoutConst
{
private:
   int m_i;
};
```

When you define a const variable globally, no memory is allocated for it; it is used by the compiler in the same way a macro is. When you define a const member variable, memory is allocated for the variable. The const is then scoped to that particular class. Thus, you can have const variables with the same name but different values for each class. When you use a const variable within a class, it is essentially a write once, read many type of a variable, because you can set its value only once but use it as many times as you would like.

Technique 73: Nonstatic consts Are Allocated in the Code Area

Category: Avoid crashes

Source

```
long la;
long lb;
TestTrig();
//Here comes trouble
const long g_lNonStaticConst = 1000;
long *plc;
```

```
plc = (long *)&g_lNonStaticConst;
*plc = 20;
```

Global nonstatic consts don't have memory associated with them. If you access the address of a global nonstatic const, space will be allocated for it in the code area, making it read only.

If you cast the address of the const to a type that is not a const, as we have done in the "Source" code listed here, you can fool the compiler into generating code that will let you overwrite the memory area. That is bad. You will most likely GP fault. Don't do this.

Looking at the map file, you can see that space was added for the const variable at the end of the code segment. (For more information on map files, check out Technique 158.)

Here is the end of the map file if we cut out the problematic code:

```
0001:0000d8dc  _SetUnhandledExceptionFilter@4 0040e8dc f kernel32:KERNEL32.dll
0001:0000d8e2  _IsBadCodePtr@4    0040e8e2 f kernel32:KERNEL32.dll
0002:00000054  ??_C@_02A@?$AA?$AA?$AA@ 0040f054 libcid:ostrint.obj
```

But once we add the problematic code, the map file is as follows:

```
0001:0000d92c  _SetUnhandledExceptionFilter@4 0040e92c f kernel32:KERNEL32.dll
0001:0000d932  _IsBadCodePtr@4    0040e932 f kernel32:KERNEL32.dll
0002:00000058  ??_C@_02A@?$AA?$AA?$AA@ 0040f058 libcid:ostrint.obj
```

You can see that segment 2 now starts four bytes further than it did before. The extra space is for the const variable. As we've mentioned previously, accessing it will do bad things. So don't.

Technique 74: Wrap Member Variables to Protect from Outside Access

Category: Avoid unexpected results; write cleaner code

Before

```
class STREAM
{
public:
    long m_lLineNumber;
    long m_ichPos;
};
```

After

```
class STREAM
{
private:
    long m_lLineNumber;
    long m_ichPos;
public:

    long STREAM::LLinePosition(void)
    {
        return m_lLineNumber;
    }
    long STREAM::LCharPosition(void)
    {
        return m_ichPos;
    }
};
```

When you make a member variable public, anyone can do anything they want with it. The class has no control over what happens to the variable. This can be dangerous. For example, in the sample code shown for this technique, some function external to the class could change the line number to −66. You have no way of making sure that the value is changed to an appropriate value. You also have no way of knowing when the value is changed and of then reacting to that change.

By contrast, if you make the member variables private, you can create accessor functions. These functions can restrict how and when the variables change. For example, the sample shown here makes the variables read only. Functions external to the class can read the values but never change them. You could also create functions for changing the variable values and perform validation or other value manipulation inside those functions. Providing such functions also means that the class always knows when a value changes and can react accordingly.

More important, making member variables private provides encapsulation. By hiding the internals, you hide the implementation from users of the class. You expose the interfaces—via the public methods—but not the implementation. You can then change the internals of the class whenever you want. In other words, the public methods are the steering wheel and the gas pedal—everyone gets to use those. The member variables and all the private functions are the mass of gadgets under the hood of the car that make the steering wheel do the right thing. Just as you wouldn't want a driver to have to mess around directly with all of the doodads inside the engine to make the car go, you don't want users of a class to have to fool with all of the doodads inside of a class to utilize its capabilities.

Technique 75: Keeping Your News Private

Category: Write cleaner code

Before

```
class RefCounted
{
public:
    ~RefCounted()
    {
    }

    RefCounted()
    {
    }

    static RefCounted *newRefCounted()
    {
        return new RefCounted;
    }
};
```

After

```
class RefCounted
{
private:
    // Made private so automatic variables can't be created.
    ~RefCounted()
    {
    }

    // Made private so object can't be created from outside
            newRefCounted
    RefCounted()
    {
    }

public:
    static RefCounted *newRefCounted()
    {
        return new RefCounted;
```

```
    }
};
```

In Chapter 3, we showed that you can create more efficient code by creating a member function that wraps new (because you avoid all of the code generated inline by new). By making your constructor private, you can force people to use your custom new function whenever they want to create objects of a particular class.

Caveat

Using this technique can cause more complexity than it is worth. If having new inlined isn't causing efficiency problems, there is no need to use this technique.

See example: RefCounted::newRefCounted() in access.cpp

Technique 76: Using Runtime Type Information

Category: Advice

Source

```
const type_info& t = typeid(&li);
cout << '\n' << t.name() << '\n' << t.raw_name() << '\n';
```

You can use runtime type information to learn about a class that is pointed to by a pointer. Type information for polymorphic classes will only be generated if the /GR compiler option is specified.

Caveat

There is significant added overhead for using runtime type information. In general, you are better off avoiding the use of runtime type information, although it can be useful for debugging purposes.

Relying on runtime type information can also get you into trouble. It is generally a bad idea to cast a pointer to a base class to a pointer to a derived class because you can very easily call nonexistent methods or access nonexistent variables. Runtime type information gives you enough information to do this somewhat safely, but it is a bad design practice. There is almost always another way to achieve the same effect. In general, avoid using dynamic_cast.

One easy way to get type information without enabling runtime type information is to derive every class from a common base class whose constructor receives type information from the derived class. This can be a debug-only thing.

See example: TextRegExp() in regexp.cpp

Technique 77: If You Allocate Memory, Override the = Operator

Category: Avoid unexpected results

Before

```
class String
{
private:
    const int m_cchTest;
    int m_cch;
    char *m_pch;
public:
    String(void) : m_cch(0), m_cchTest(10)
    {
        m_pch = NULL;
    }

    ~String(void)
    {
        if(m_pch)
            delete m_pch;
    }

};
```

After

```
class String
{
private:
    const int m_cchTest;
    int m_cch;
    char *m_pch;
    void InitString(const char *pch, int cch);
    void ReinitString(const char *pch, int cch);
public:
    String(void) : m_cch(0), m_cchTest(10)
    {
        m_pch = NULL;
    }
```

```
~String(void)
{
    if(m_pch)
        delete m_pch;
}

const String& operator=(const String &string)
{
    if(&string != this)
        ReinitString(string.m_pch, string.m_cch);
    return *this;
}

const String& operator=(const char *sz)
{
    ReinitString(sz, strlen(sz));
    return *this;
}

};
```

Both the copy constructor and the = operator are supplied automatically by the compiler. If you allocate memory within your class (or rather, if you allocate memory that persists with the class—not memory that you temporarily create and destroy within function boundaries), you will then need to create a copy constructor and override the = operator. Why? The default constructor and = operator will not copy over the memory that you have allocated. They will merely copy over the pointer.

For example, consider the "Before" sample code for this technique. The class has a member variable called m_pch that contains a pointer to a character buffer. The default = operator will copy over the pointer. But it will not copy over the buffer itself. Thus, you end up with two pointers pointing to the same area of memory. When one of these classes is destroyed, the memory will be freed. Furthermore, the other class will then be unusable because it is now pointing to memory that has been freed. Instead, you need a copy of the memory pointed to as well. By overriding the = operator, you can create member functions that will produce a new memory buffer and copy over the contents.

Also see Technique 94. The same issues discussed here apply to the copy constructor.

See example: class String in string.cpp

Technique 78: Guard against Self-Referential Operators

Category: Avoid unexpected results; write faster code

Before

```
const String& operator=(const String &string)
{
    ReinitString(string.m_pch, string.m_cch);
    return *this;
}
```

After

```
const String& operator=(const String &string)
{
    if(&string != this)
        ReinitString(string.m_pch, string.m_cch);
    return *this;
}
```

Remember that an operator can operate on itself. For example, one could have code such as the following:

```
x = x;
```

You need to check for this case before your operator does its thing. For example, suppose your operator frees up the memory of the operand on the left and copies over the memory from the operand on the right. You'd end up freeing the memory before you copied it. Oops!

Suppose, instead, that your operator made a copy of the right operand and then copied it over to the left operand. Well, you just did a whole bunch of unnecessary allocation (especially if you were copying a 25M bitmap).

Instead, check to make sure that the right operand is not the same as the left operand by comparing it to the this pointer, as shown in the "After" code for this technique.

See example: String = operator in string.cpp

Technique 79: Too Much Parameter Checking Is Still Too Much

Category: Write faster and cleaner code

Before

```
class Caution {
private:
   int  m_nCount;
public:
   Caution(void) : m_nCount(1)
   {
   }

   void SetCount(int nVal)
   {
      if (nVal <= 0)
         m_nCount = 1;
      else
         m_nCount = nVal;
   }

   int DoSomething(int nVal) {
      if (m_nCount > 0)
         return nVal % m_nCount;
      else
         return 0;
   }
}
```

After

```
class Caution {
private:
   int  m_nCount;
public:
   Caution(void) : m_nCount(1)
   {
   }

   void SetCount(int nVal)
```

```
{
    if (nVal <= 0)
        m_nCount = 1;
    else
        m_nCount = nVal;
}

int DoSomething(int nVal) {
    return nVal % m_nCount;
}
}
```

Checking parameters is important. But checking parameters also takes time. So you should only check when you need to, such as in public member functions. Consider the code shown for this technique. The class has a private member variable with an accessor function. The variable (m_nCount) is initialized by the constructor, and the range of the variable is controlled by the accessor function. Thus, you can be guaranteed that m_nCount will not get set to 0 or less from the outside. Because DoSomething guards against m_nCount being less than 0, the check is unnecessary. In a more complex example, the class may have several private functions. Depending on what the private functions do, they may not need to do parameter validity checking, especially if the public functions that call them already do validity checking.

Caveat

When in doubt, err on the side of doing too much checking. You can also add asserts to your code.

Technique 80: Creating const Operators

Category: Compile your code

Before

```
class String {
    char & operator[](int i)
    {
        return m_pch[i];
    }

};
```

```
void PrintConstString(const String &string)
{
   int i = 0;
   while(string[i])
   {
      cout << string[i];
      i++;
   }
}
```

After

```
class String {
   char & operator[](int i)
   {
      return m_pch[i];
   }
   const char& operator[](int i) const
   {
      return m_pch[i];
   }

};

void PrintConstString(const String &string)
{
   int i = 0;
   while(string[i])
   {
      cout << string[i];

      // The commented line won't compile!
      //string[i] = ' ';
      i++;
   }
}
```

When you declare that an argument is const, you protect it from being changed within a function. If you create operators, you may wish to create operators that handle const expressions as well. For example, consider the "Before" code listed here. In the function PrintConstString we call the [ ] operator on a const String. But we haven't created a [ ] operator that takes a const operand. As a result, we get a compiler error on the following line:

```
while(string[i])
```

Why did we get an error? Because we've attempted to apply the [ ] operator to a const String when there is no operator for doing so.

In the "After" code, we've created an [ ] operator that can handle const operands, and the code now compiles.

Remember that declaring a variable as const means that the compiler will give an error if you try to change it. Thus, if you try code such as the following, which would in fact change the value of a const, you'll get a compiler error:

```
string[i] = ' ';
```

See example: String::operator[ ] and PrintConstString( ) in string.cpp

Technique 81: Private Derivation

Category: Write cleaner code

Before

```
template <class T>
class Stack : public Drg <T>
{
};
```

After

```
template <class T>
class Stack : private Drg <T>
{
};
```

When you derive from a class using the public access modifier, all public members of the base class are available to users of the derived class. On the other hand, if you derive using the private access modifier, then none of the members of the base class are visible outside of the derived class. This lets the derived class use the functionality of the base class without exposing the base class's interfaces. Instead, the derived class can decide exactly what interfaces to expose.

By being able to use all of the capabilities of a base class of functionality without exposing all of that functionality to the user of the class, you can essentially create classes that provide core private functionality, from which you can build customized classes.

For example, consider the class Stack. This is a general-purpose stack class, built on the generic array management capabilities of the Drg class. Although it uses all of the Drg capabilities internally, it doesn't expose them. Rather, it only exposes the stack-related interfaces. As a result, the class gets to reuse a powerful set of code without exposing the mess to the Stack user.

Private derivation, in many respects, gives you the same capability as embedding a class and delegating to it. That is, we could have embedded the Drg class within the Stack class.

Technique 82: Making Sure a Class or Structure Size Stays within Bounds

Category: Write faster code; avoid unexpected results

Before

```
//A DWORD structure for storing info
class FixedSize
{
    DWORD dwRes1:4;
    DWORD dwRes2:4;
    DWORD fRes3:1;
    DWORD fRes4:1;
    DWORD dwUnused:23;
};
```

After

```
//A DWORD structure for storing info
class FixedSize
{
    DWORD dwRes1:4;
    DWORD dwRes2:4;
    DWORD fRes3:1;
    DWORD fRes4:1;
    DWORD dwUnused:23;
};
#ifdef _DEBUG
char szFixedSizeAssert[sizeof(DWORD)-sizeof(FixedSize)+1];
#endif //DEBUG
```

There are many times when you want a structure or class to fit within a particular size. For example, you may have a class for nodes in a tree or some other type of data structure and want to make sure the nodes are kept within a particular size either for alignment purposes or to make sure memory usage does not become large. In the "Before" code for this technique, you can see that we've set up a structure in a DWORD. We plan on allocating a few hundred thousand of these structures, so we want to make sure the structure doesn't get larger than a DWORD in size as we add new bit fields or members to it.

Note, however, that if you count up the number of bits in the structure, we made a mistake in the dwUnused portion. The entire structure is 33 bits—larger than the 32 bits in a DWORD. So even though our handy comment told us we were clever about how we defined our structure, we made an error.

The "After" code catches the expanded size by using a nice trick. We allocate an array and set the number of elements in that array to the desired size of the structure minus the actual size of the structure. If the structure is larger than the desired size, we would then be trying to allocate an array of size 0 or less. (For example, in our case, sizeof(FixedSize) is 5, so 4 – 5 + 1 = 0.) That causes a compiler error. If, on the other hand, the structure is the desired size, we'll allocate an array of length 1 and not have an error.

Note that we put this check only during debug compilation; by doing so, we don't introduce the array structure into our retail code.

See example: class FixedSize in regexp.cpp

Technique 83: Use Inheritance instead of Unions

Category: Avoid crashes and unexpected results

Before

```
class uClass
{
public:
    uClass() : nTeacherId(0), fltSalary(0.)
    {
    }


    char *szName;
    float fltSalary;
    union
    {
        int nTeacherId;
```

```
        int nStaffId;
    };
};

int main(int argc, char* argv[])
{
    uClass c1;

    cout << c1.nTeacherId << endl;

    return 0;
}
```

After

```
class baseClass {
public:
    baseClass() : fltSalary(0.)
    {
    }


    char *szName;
    float fltSalary;
};

class teacherClass : public baseClass {
public:
    teacherClass() : nTeacherId(0)
    {
    }

    int nTeacherId;
};

class staffClass : public baseClass {
public:
    staffClass() : nStaffId(3)
    {
    }

    int nStaffId;
};
```

```
int main(int argc, char* argv[])
{
    teacherClass t1;
    staffClass s1;

    cout << t1.nTeacherId << endl;
    cout << s1.nStaffId << endl;

    return 0;
}
```

Unions don't give you type safety. Any member in the union can appear at any time. So if you are storing different values depending on the type of object you have, there is no way of verifying that the right member is being accessed for a particular object.

For example, in the "Before" code for this technique, we have a class that stores employee information. If the information is about a teacher, it has a teacher ID. If it is about staff, it has a staff ID. Because a person is either a staff member or a teacher, we saved some space by combining both possible values into a union.

Although we could add a flag to indicate whether the employee is staff or a teacher, the compiler will not make sure that we only access the nTeacherId variable for teachers. The compiler doesn't care. If we forget to check what type of an item we have, pandemonium could break out.

By contrast, consider the "After" code, in which we have created a base class with the members common between all classes. We then derive from that class to create a class just for teachers and a class just for staff. Although there is minimal-size overhead to this approach, we do get type safety. The compiler will prevent us from trying to access an nStaffId from a teacher or an nTeacherId from a staff member.

Technique 84: Be Careful with Initialization When You Use Unions

Category: Avoid unexpected results

Before

```
class uClass
{
public:
    uClass() : nTeacherId(0), fltSalary(0.), nStaffId(3)
    {
    }
```

```
    char *szName;
    float fltSalary;
    union
    {
        int nTeacherId;
        int nStaffId;
    };
};

int main(int argc, char* argv[])
{
    uClass   c1;

    cout << c1.nTeacherId;
    return 0;
}
```

After

```
class uClass
{
public:
    uClass() : nStaffId(3), fltSalary(0.)
    {
    }


    char *szName;
    float fltSalary;
    union
    {
        int nTeacherId;
        int nStaffId;
    };
};

int main(int argc, char* argv[])
{
    uClass   c1;

    cout << c1.nTeacherId;
    return 0;
}
```

When you have unions, you can initialize any of the members in the union by name. If you look at the "Before" code for this technique, you can see that we've initialized the nTeacherId and the nStaffId to different values. However, both of these refer to the same variable. Thus, it is the second initialization value that will apply. If you don't notice that you have a union, you could be very surprised by the result when you go to examine a variable within the union.

Technique 85: Don't Cast to a Derived Class

Category: Avoid crashes and unexpected results

Source

```
class base
{
public:
    base() : nSize(4)
    {
    }

    int nSize;
};

class deriv : private base
{
public:
    deriv() : nSize2(2)
    {
    }

    int nSize2;

    int getSize()
    {
        return nSize2;
    }
};


int main(int argc, char* argv[])
{
    base *b = new base;
    deriv *d = new deriv;
```

```
//This is OK
cout << ((base *) d)->nSize << endl;
//This isn't
cout << ((deriv *) b)->getSize() << endl;

return 0;
}
```

It's okay to cast from a derived class to a base class. All of the capabilities of the base class are present in the derived class. By contrast, it is not okay to cast from a base class to a derived class. Derived classes quite often have extra members and variables that base classes do not. You can easily end up referring to or overwriting variables that don't exist and generally wreaking havoc.

In the "Source" code shown for this technique, for example, the second cout will print garbage to the screen. The getSize member function and the member variable it uses are not part of the base class. Although the compiler will grab the code from where it stores the derived class, the variable nSize2 does not exist in the base class. Depending on the size difference between the base class and the derived class, you could also get an access violation rather than garbage.

Technique 86: Be Very Careful when Using Member Variables after Deleting this

Category: Avoid crashes and unexpected results

Before

```
int Release()
{
    int cRef;

    if(!(--m_cRef))
        delete this;
    return m_cRef;
}
```

After

```
int Release()
{
    int cRef;
```

```
    --m_cRef;
    cRef = m_cRef;
    if(!cRef)
        delete this;
    return cRef;
}
```

Deleting the this pointer calls the class destructor. Afterward, member variables are in an unknown state. If you need to use member variables after you've deleted the this pointer, first store them in local variables and then do the delete.

See example: RefCounted::Release() in access.cpp

CHAPTER 7

Abstract Base Classes

USING ABSTRACT BASE CLASSES LETS YOU SET UP a structure for a class and forces users of that class to provide implementations.

Technique 87: The Compiler Checks for Instantiation of Abstract Base Classes

Category: Compile your code

Source

```
class Interface1
{
public:
    virtual void SetInt(int i) PURE;
    virtual void PrintInt(void) PURE;
    virtual void SetFloat1(float f) PURE;
    virtual void PrintFloat1(void) PURE;
};

class Interface2
{
public:
    virtual void SetInt(int i) PURE;
    virtual void PrintInt(void) PURE;
    virtual void SetFloat2(float f) PURE;
    virtual void PrintFloat2(void)
    {
        printf("15.5 from derived ");
    }
};

class Derived : public Interface1, public Interface2
{
private:
    int     m_i;
```

```
        float    m_f1;
        float    m_f2;
public:
    Derived() : m_i(0), m_f1(0.0f), m_f2(0.555f)
    {
    }
    void SetInt(int i)
    {
        m_i = i;
    }
    void PrintInt(void)
    {
        printf("%d ", m_i);
    }
    void SetFloat2(float f)
    {
        m_f2 = f;
    }
    void PrintFloat2(void)
    {
        printf("%f ", m_f2);
    }
    void SetFloat1(float f)
    {
        m_f1 = f;
    }
    void PrintFloat1(void)
    {
        printf("%f ", m_f1);
    }
    void PrintLF(void)
    {
        printf("\n");
    }
};

void TestABC(void)
{
    Derived d;
    Interface1 *pif1 = &d;
    Interface2 *pif2 = &d;
    //The following line will cause a lot of errors
    Interface1 if1;
```

```
        d.SetInt(10);
        d.SetFloat1(1.5);
        d.SetFloat2(2.5);
        d.PrintInt();
        d.PrintFloat1();
        d.PrintFloat2();
        d.PrintLF();
        pif1->PrintInt();
        pif1->PrintFloat1();
        d.PrintLF();
        pif2->PrintInt();
        pif2->PrintFloat2();
        d.PrintLF();
}
```

Abstract base classes do not contain implementation. Rather, classes derived from the abstract base class must provide the implementation for the pure virtual functions in the abstract base class. If you try to create a class for which implementation has not been defined, the compiler will complain loudly.

For example, in TestABC(), we have the following line:

```
Interface1 if1;
```

This line will cause the following errors and warnings because Interface1 is an abstract base class:

```
C:\book\inherit2\inherit2.h(127) : error C2259: 'Interface1' : cannot instantiate
abstract class due to following members:
C:\book\inherit2\inherit2.h(127) : warning C4259: 'void Interface1::SetInt(int)' :
pure virtual function was not defined
C:\book\inherit2\inherit2.h(127) : warning C4259: 'void
Interface1::PrintInt(void)' : pure virtual function was not defined
C:\book\inherit2\inherit2.h(127) : warning C4259: 'void
Interface1::SetFloat1(float)' : pure virtual function was not defined
C:\book\inherit2\inherit2.h(127) : warning C4259: 'void
Interface1::PrintFloat1(void)' : pure virtual function was not defined
```

By contrast, errors are not generated by creating Derived or by creating interface pointers that point to Derived classes because the Derived class provides implementation for all of the pure virtual functions in the abstract base class.

See example: TestABC() in inherit2.h

Technique 88: Base Classes Can Be Designed to Assume That Derived Classes Provide Implementation

Category: Write cleaner code

Source

```
class Shape
{
private:
    int m_xLeft;
    int m_yTop;
    int m_xRight;
    int m_yBottom;
protected:
    virtual void Draw(int x1, int y1, int x2, int y2) = 0;
public:
    Shape(int x1, int y1, int x2, int y2) : m_xLeft(x1), m_yTop(y1),
      m_xRight(x2), m_yBottom(y2)
    {
    }
    Shape()
    {
    }
    // Render the primitive with an offset as given by x and y below and a scale
    // factor of mx in x direction and my in y
    // Scaling is applied around the mid point of the bounding box. offset is
    // from the top right.
    void Render(int xOffset, int yOffset, int mx, int my)
    {
        int x1;
        int y1;
        int dx;
        int dy;

        x1 = m_xLeft + xOffset;
        y1 = m_yTop + yOffset;
        dx = (m_xRight - m_xLeft)*mx;
        dy = (m_yBottom - m_yTop)*mx;
        Draw(x1, y1, x1 + dx, y1 + dy);
    }
};
```

```
class Rectangle : public Shape
{
private:
    void Draw(int x1, int y1, int x2, int y2)
    {
        cout << "Rectangle("<<x1<<" ,"<<y1<<" ,"<<x2<<" ,"<<y2<<")";
    }
public:
    Rectangle(int x1, int y1, int x2, int y2) : Shape(x1, y1, x2, y2)
    {
    }
};

class Circle : public Shape
{
private:
    void Draw(int x1, int y1, int x2, int y2)
    {
        cout << "Circle("<<x1<<" ,"<<y1<<" ,"<<x2<<" ,"<<y2<<")";
    }
public:
    Circle(int x1, int y1, int x2, int y2) : Shape(x1, y1, x2, y2)
    {
    }
};
```

Base classes provide generic functionality for objects. You don't need to know any implementation details when you create a base class. As long as you know the various interfaces an object will have, you can create an abstract base class. The classes derived from the abstract base class provide the implementation.

For example, the "Source" code for this technique uses a generic class called Shape. It has some methods and variables, including a method for rendering the shape. Note, however, that Render doesn't know how to draw any particular shapes. Rather, it calls a pure virtual function called Draw. All classes derived from Shape must provide implementation for the Draw method.

Because Draw is a pure virtual function, classes derived from Shape must provide an implementation for Draw ; otherwise they cannot be instantiated.

See example: class Shape, RoundedRect, Circle, and Rectangle in inherit1.h

Technique 89: vtables Use Space

Category: Write faster code

Source

```
class Derived : public Interface1, public Interface2
{
private:
    int     m_i;
    float   m_f1;
    float   m_f2;
public:
    Derived() : m_i(0), m_f1(0.0f), m_f2(0.555f)
    {
    }
};


class NotDerived
{
private:
    int     m_i;
    float   m_f1;
    float   m_f2;
public:
    NotDerived() : m_i(0), m_f1(0.0f), m_f2(0.555f)
    {
    }
};


void TestABC(void)
{

    printf("Derived size = %d\n", sizeof(Derived) );
    printf("Not Derived size = %d\n", sizeof(NotDerived) );
}
```

Note that vtables consume four bytes per class instance. For the "Source" example shown for this technique, the Derived class consumes 20 bytes, whereas the NotDerived class consumes 12 bytes. The difference is caused by the two classes from which Derived inherits.

See example: class Derived in inherit2.h

Technique 90: Multiple Inheritance from Abstract Base Classes Does Not Cause Ambiguities

Category: Compile your code

Source

```cpp
class Interface1
{
public:
   virtual void PrintInt(void) = 0;
};
class Interface2
{
public:
   virtual void PrintInt(void) = 0;
};
class Derived : public Interface1, public Interface2
{
private:
   int     m_i;
   float   m_f1;
   float   m_f2;
public:
   Derived() : m_i(0), m_f1(0.0f), m_f2(0.555f)
   {
   }

   void PrintInt(void)
   {
      printf("%d ", m_i);
   }
};
void TestABC(void)
{
   Derived d;
   Interface1 *pif1 = &d;
   Interface2 *pif2 = &d;
   d.PrintInt();
   pif1->PrintInt();
   pif2->PrintInt();
}
```

The Derived class is inherited from two base classes. Each base class has a PrintInt method defined on it. Thus, one might think that the d.PrintInt() line in TestABC would be ambiguous. There is, in fact, no ambiguity, because the PrintInt methods in Interface1 and Interface2 are pure virtual methods.

Let's take a look at the actual code that is generated. We'll begin by taking a look at the PrintInt method in Derived:

```
44:       void PrintInt(void)
45:       {
00401550  push          ebp
00401551  mov           ebp,esp
00401553  push          ecx
00401554  mov           dword ptr [ebp-4],ecx
46:           printf("%d ", m_i);
00401557  mov           eax,dword ptr [this]
0040155A  mov           ecx,dword ptr [eax+8]
0040155D  push          ecx
0040155E  push          offset ??_C@_03CPCE@?$CFd?5?$AA@(0x00415a30)
00401563  call          printf(0x00401b70)
00401568  add           esp,8
47:       }
0040156B  mov           esp,ebp
0040156D  pop           ebp
0040156E  ret
```

Now let's take a look at the code in TestABC. The function d.PrintInt() calls into the jump table at 0x401055:

```
79:       d.PrintInt();
00401224  lea           ecx,dword ptr [d]
00401227  call          @ILT+85(?PrintInt@Derived@@UAEXXZ)(0x00401055)
```

This call is to a jump to the PrintInt function in Derived:

```
00401055  jmp           Derived::PrintInt(0x00401550)
```

Because the interface pif1 is the first base class for Derived, it behaves the same as the this pointer for Derived. Here's what happens when we call PrintInt from the pif1 pointer:

```
83:       pif1->PrintInt();
00401244  mov           ecx,dword ptr [pif1]
00401247  mov           edx,dword ptr [ecx]
```

```
00401249   mov        ecx,dword ptr [pif1]
0040124C   call       dword ptr [edx+4]
```

Because pif2 is the second base class for Derived, it's four bytes away from the this pointer for Derived. The compiler fixes up the this pointer by calling out to the jump table at 0x401AB0 (Derived::Print), as you can see in the following assembly. The jump table fixes up ecx before calling out to PrintInt:

```
86:        pif2->PrintInt();
00401262   mov        eax,dword ptr [pif2]
00401265   mov        edx,dword ptr [eax]
00401267   mov        ecx,dword ptr [pif2]
0040126A   call       dword ptr [edx+4]


00401082   jmp         Derived::PrintInt(0x00401ab0)
```

Here's what gets called:

```
Derived::PrintInt:
00401AB0   sub        ecx,4
00401AB3   jmp        @ILT+85(?PrintInt@Derived@@UAEXXZ)(0x00401055)
```

See example: TestABC() in inherit2.h
See also: Technique 100

CHAPTER 8
Constructors

WHEN YOU CREATE A CLASS, YOU SHOULD BE SURE to create a constructor for it. In this chapter, you'll learn some techniques to employ with your constructors. For example, you'll learn how to use default arguments to reduce the number of constructors you create. You'll also learn about virtual destructors, as well as many other things.

Technique 91: Initialize Your Member Variables

Category: Avoid unexpected results

Before

```
class String
{
private:
   const int m_cchTest;
   int m_cch;
   char *m_pch;
};
```

After

```
class String
{
private:
   const int m_cchTest;
   int m_cch;
   char *m_pch;
public:
   String(void) : m_cch(0), m_cchTest(10), m_pch(NULL)
   {
   }
};
```

We've gone over this several times before, but it's worth repeating. Always initialize member variables. That way, they are in a known state before they get used. This is a fundamental practice that you need to follow. As soon as you declare a variable in a class definition, add the code for initializing it.

There are two approaches for initializing variables: using initialization lists and using code inside the constructor. In general, it is best to use initialization lists because they are more efficient.

See example: class String in string.cpp
See also: Techniques 69, 70, and 71

Technique 92: Default Arguments Let You Reduce the Number of Constructors

Category: Write cleaner code; avoid stupid mistakes

Before

```
class Drgbase
{
private:
    long    m_lcbSize;
    long    m_lcbChunk;
public:
    Drgbase(void)
    {
        m_lcbSize = 4;
        m_lcbChunk = 48;
    }

    Drgbase(long lcbSize)
    {
        m_lcbSize = lcbSize;
        m_lcbChunk = lcChunk * 12;
    }

    Drgbase(long lcbSize, long lcChunk)
    {
        m_lcbSize = lcbSize;
        m_lcbChunk = lcChunk * lcbSize;
    }
};
```

After

```
class Drgbase
{
private:
    long    m_lcbSize;
    long    m_lcbChunk;
public:
    Drgbase(long lcbSize=4, long lcChunk=12)
    {
        m_lcbSize = lcbSize;
        m_lcbChunk = lcChunk * lcbSize;
    }
};
```

Using default arguments is a nice way to reduce the number of constructors you need. For example, in the "Before" code for this technique, we allow the user to construct the class by passing in zero, one, or two parameters. To deal with this, we've created three constructors.

Note, however, that this means there are three different methods that need to be coordinated. If we change the algorithm used in one, we need to make sure that we change the algorithm used in all of them. (Sure, we could create a private function used by the constructors to do some centralization. Likewise, we really should have declared constants for the various values so that they'd be less likely to get out of synch among the various constructors. But, we're trying to prove a point.)

By contrast, look at the "After" code. In this case, we've used default arguments to reduce from three constructors to one constructor. We have less code and less chance for screwups, and the code is also more elegant and easier to read.

Caveat

Note that when you use default arguments, and you don't supply all of the arguments, they are always filled in from left to right. You can't tell the compiler to use the default for the first argument and some supplied value for the second argument, as you can with VBScript.

See example: class Drgbase in drg.h

Technique 93: Making Constructors Private

Category: Write cleaner code

Before

```
class String
{
private:
   const int m_cchTest;
   int m_cch;
   char *m_pch;
   void InitString(const char *pch, int cch);
public:
   String(void) : m_cch(0), m_cchTest(10)
   {
      m_pch = NULL;
   }

   String(const String &string): m_cchTest(10)
   {
      InitString(string.m_pch, string.m_cch);
   }

   String(char *sz): m_cchTest(10)
   {
      InitString(sz, strlen(sz));
   }

   ~String(void)
   {
      if(m_pch)
         delete m_pch;
   }
};
```

After

```
class String
{
private:
   const int m_cchTest;
   int m_cch;
   char *m_pch;
   void InitString(const char *pch, int cch);
```

```
    String(const String &string): m_cchTest(10)
    {
        InitString(string.m_pch, string.m_cch);
    }

    String(char *sz): m_cchTest(10)
    {
        InitString(sz, strlen(sz));
    }

public:
    String(void) : m_cch(0), m_cchTest(10)
    {
        m_pch = NULL;
    }


    ~String(void)
    {
        if(m_pch)
            delete m_pch;
    }
};
```

You can control access to constructors by making them private. For example, in the "After" code shown for this technique, the copy constructor is only available to member functions of the class; code outside cannot perform copies.

For even more control, you can make the constructor private. Then, the only way for users to create the class would be through special public functions you write explicitly for that purpose.

See example: RefCounted::newRefCounted() in access.cpp

Technique 94: If You Allocate Memory, Create a Copy Constructor

Category: Avoid unexpected results

Before

```
class String
{
```

```
private:
    const int m_cchTest;
    int m_cch;
    char *m_pch;
public:
    String(void) : m_cch(0), m_cchTest(10)
    {
        m_pch = NULL;
    }


    ~String(void)
    {
        if(m_pch)
            delete m_pch;
    }


};
```

After

```
class String
{
private:
    const int m_cchTest;
    int m_cch;
    char *m_pch;
    void InitString(const char *pch, int cch);
public:
    String(void) : m_cch(0), m_cchTest(10)
    {
        m_pch = NULL;
    }


    String(const String &string): m_cchTest(10)
    {
        InitString(string.m_pch, string.m_cch);
    }


    String(char *sz): m_cchTest(10)
    {
        InitString(sz, strlen(sz));
    }
```

```
    ~String(void)
    {
        if(m_pch)
            delete m_pch;
    }
};
```

Both the copy constructor and the = operator are supplied automatically by the compiler. If you allocate memory within your class (or rather, if you allocate memory that persists with the class—not memory that you temporarily create and destroy within function boundaries), you will then need to create a copy constructor and override the = operator. This is because the default constructor and = operator will not copy over the memory that you have allocated. They will merely copy over the pointer.

For example, consider the "Before" sample code for this technique. The class has a member variable called m_pch that contains a pointer to a character buffer. The default copy constructor will copy over the pointer. But it will not copy over the buffer itself. Thus, you end up with two pointers pointing to the same area of memory. Instead, you need a copy of the memory pointed to as well. By creating a copy constructor, you can create member functions that will create a new memory buffer and copy over the contents.

Also see Technique 77. The same issues discussed here apply to the = operator.

See example: class String in string.cpp

Technique 95: If You Create a Copy Constructor, Remember to Copy Over Allocated Memory

Category: Avoid unexpected results

Before

```
class String
{
private:
    const int m_cchTest;
    int m_cch;
    char *m_pch;
public:
    String(void) : m_cch(0), m_cchTest(10)
    {
        m_pch = NULL;
    }
```

```
        ~String(void)
        {
            if(m_pch)
                delete m_pch;
        }

};
```

After

```
class String
{
private:
    const int m_cchTest;
    int m_cch;
    char *m_pch;
    void InitString(const char *pch, int cch);
public:
    String(void) : m_cch(0), m_cchTest(10)
    {
        m_pch = NULL;
    }

    String(const String &string): m_cchTest(10)
    {
        InitString(string.m_pch, string.m_cch);
    }

    String(char *sz): m_cchTest(10)
    {
        InitString(sz, strlen(sz));
    }

    ~String(void)
    {
        if(m_pch)
            delete m_pch;
    }
};
```

```
void String::InitString(const char * pch, int cch)
{
    m_cch = 0;
    m_pch = NULL;
    if(cch)
    {
        m_pch = new char[cch+1];
        if(m_pch)
        {
            strcpy(m_pch, pch);
            m_cch = cch;
        }
    }
}
```

This technique isn't much different from the previous one. Are we repeating ourselves senselessly? Nope. The point is important. The default action of a copy constructor is to copy over the member variables. If any of the variables are pointers, you should make a copy of the memory that is pointed to and then set the pointer to that memory. That will make a true copy. Otherwise, you end up with a partial copy: the simple types are copies that you can modify; the pointed to memory is now shared between two (or more) objects.

See example: class String in string.cpp

Technique 96: If You Expect to Inherit, Make Destructors Virtual

Category: Avoid unexpected results

Before

```
class base2
{
public:
    base2(base2 &b2)
    {
        cout << "base2 copy ctor\n";
    }
    base2()
    {
        cout << "base2 constructor\n";
    }
}
```

```
    ~base2()
    {
        cout << "base2 destructor\n";
    }
};

class Derived2 : public base2
{
public:
    ~Derived2()
    {
        cout << "Derived2 destructor\n";
    }
};
```

After

```
class base2
{
public:
    base2(base2 &b2)
    {
        cout << "base2 copy ctor\n";
    }
    base2()
    {
        cout << "base2 constructor\n";
    }
    virtual ~base2()
    {
        cout << "base2 destructor\n";
    }
};

class Derived2 : public base2
{
public:
    ~Derived2()
    {
        cout << "Derived2 destructor\n";
    }
};
```

If you ever expect your class to be inherited, make the destructor virtual. If you don't plan to have a destructor because you have nothing to clean up, create one with an empty body and make it virtual.

Why bother? Remember that you can use pointers to base classes to manipulate derived classes. Consider the class Derived2 shown in this section's "Before" example. As you can see, it inherits from base2. Consider the following code:

```
Derived2    *pd2;
pd2 = new Derived2;
delete pd2;
```

Here, we create and delete a pointer to the derived class. Everything will work fine: both the derived and base class will be deleted.

Suppose that, instead, you did the following:

```
Derived2    *pd2;
base2    *pdb;
pd2 = new Derived2;
pdb = (base2 *) pd2;
delete pdb;
```

In this new code, we've cast the pointer to the base class and we delete that pointer. Well, the destructor wasn't virtual. So in this case, the destructor for the base class (base2) gets called, but the destructor for the derived class that is pointed to (Derived2) is not called. Not good!

By contrast, in the "After" code, base2 's destructor is virtual. When code such as that just shown is executed, both the Derived2 and base2 destructors will be called.

Now, you may look at the sample code here and argue that it is completely contrived. It really isn't. Quite often, functions are written that take pointers to base classes and rely on virtual functions to do the right thing. After all, doing so allows you to write a generic function that can handle a variety of different derived classes. Such functions may call delete. And if they do, you will see this problem. For example, the code could look like this:

```
Derived2    *pd2;
base2    *pdb;
pd2 = new Derived2;
Process(pd2);

void Process(base2 *pbase2)
{
    //Do some stuff here...
    delete pbase2;
}
```

The code seems innocuous. Looking it over, you may not even have noticed the cast and the hidden danger lurking within.

In summary, if the destructor isn't virtual, then the destructor for the base class will be called, but not for the derived class. Something bad will most likely happen.

See example: TestVirtualDTor() in inherit.cpp

Technique 97: If You Have Multiple Constructors, Be Explicit about Which One to Use

Category: Avoid unexpected results

Before

```
class Derived1 : public base1
{
public:
    Derived1(Derived1 &derived1)
    {
        cout << "Derived1 copy ctor\n";
    }
    Derived1()
    {
        cout << "Derived1 constructor\n";
    }
};


Derived1     d1(*pd1);
```

After

```
class Derived1 : public base1
{
public:
    Derived1(Derived1 &derived1) : base1(derived1)
    {
        cout << "Derived1 copy ctor\n";
    }
```

```
    Derived1()
    {
        cout << "Derived1 constructor\n";
    }
};
```

```
Derived1    d1(*pd1);
```

If you don't specify which constructor to use, the compiler will automatically choose the default constructor. Often, that isn't what you want, especially when inheritance is involved. For example, consider the "Before" code for this technique. Here, Derived1 comes from base1. There are two constructors in Derived1: a default constructor and a copy constructor. The code fragment that creates the class d1 explicitly calls the copy constructor. What happens?

First, the copy constructor for Derived1 is called. That implicitly calls the constructor for base1. Which one? The default, of course. So, while we called the copy constructor for the derived class, we don't call the copy constructor for the base class. As you have seen in other techniques, this can lead to problems, especially if the class allocates memory. (See, for example, Technique 94 in this chapter.) By contrast, look at the "After" code. Here, the copy constructor for Derived1 explicitly calls the copy constructor for the base class. Thus, when d1 is created, the copy constructor for Derived1 is called, and then the copy constructor for base1 is called. Any copying that the base class needs to do is properly handled.

See example: TestVirtualDTor in inherit.cpp

Inheritance

INHERITANCE IS ONE OF THE GREAT ASPECTS of C++ programming. We use it all of the time for encapsulation, reuse, and more. This chapter provides some techniques relating to inheritance.

Technique 98: IsA versus HasA

Category: Write cleaner code

Source

```
class IsA : public base
{
public:
   IsA() : base()
   {
   }
   int GetI1()
   {
      return base::GetI1()+5;
   }
   int GetI2()
   {
      return base::GetI2()+5;
   }
};

class HasA
{
private:
   base _b;
public:
   HasA() : _b()
   {
   }
   int GetI1()
```

```
        {
            return _b.GetI1()+20;
        }
        int GetI2()
        {
            return 20;
        }
};
```

IsA relationships are inheritance relationships. They are used when some class expands on or specializes some other class. For example, pizza is a type of food. Like all food objects, it provides calories when consumed. But it also has extra characteristics that are not common to all food objects, such as being great cold for breakfast.

HasA relationships are containment relationships. They are used when some class utilizes but does not modify capabilities of an object. For example, a car has an engine and wheels. The car object is created by combining together several other objects. But these objects are not extended or overridden by the container object, the car. Furthermore, the engine and wheels may not even be exposed outside of the car object. HasA relationships are established by creating member variables.

See example: inherit1.h

Technique 99: Scoping Rules

Category: Write cleaner code

Source

```
class base
{
    private:
        int i1;
        int i2;
    public:
        base() : i1(10), i2(20)
        {
        }
        int GetI1(void) { return i1;}
    protected:
        int GetI2(void) { return i2;}
};
```

```cpp
class DerivedPub : public base
{
public:
   DerivedPub() : base()
   {
   }
   int GetI1()
   {
      return base::GetI1()+5;
   }
   int GetI2()
   {
      return base::GetI2()+5;
   }
};

class DerivedPriv : private base
{
public:
   DerivedPriv() : base()
   {
   }
   int GetI1()
   {
      return base::GetI1()+10;
   }
   int GetI2()
   {
      return base::GetI2()+10;
   }
};

class HasA
{
private:
   base _b;
public:
   HasA() : _b()
   {
   }
   int GetI1()
   {
      return _b.GetI1()+20;
   }
```

```
      int GetI2()
      {
         return 20;
      }
};

class DerivedProt : protected base
{
public:
   DerivedProt() : base()
   {
   }
};
class DerivedProt2 : protected DerivedProt
{
public:
   DerivedProt2() : DerivedProt()
   {
   }
   int GetI1()
   {
      return base::GetI1()+30;
   }
   int GetI2()
   {
      return base::GetI2()+30;
   }
};
```

You can use the public, protected, and private access modifiers when you
list the classes from which a particular class is derived. These perform different
roles, as shown in Table 9.1. The first column in the table indicates the access
modifier used when inheriting. The next two columns indicate how an item from
the base class will behave in the inherited class. For example, as the first row
shows, when public inheritance is used, public members of the base class appear
as public members in the derived class:

Know which type of inheritance is required. With public inheritance, all the
public members of the base are publicly accessible to the derived-class users. Protected members of base are only accessible to the derived-class member functions.

With protected inheritance, all the public and protected members of the base
class are available only to the derived class. Users of the derived class can't know
anything about the base class. This hides the implementation and interfaces of
the base class from users of the derived class.

Table 9.1   Effect of Inheritance Modifier

INHERITANCE MODIFIER	BECOME IN THE BASE CLASS MEMBERS	DERIVED CLASS
public	public	public
public	protected	protected
public	private	not accessible
protected	public	protected
protected	protected	protected
protected	private	not accessible
private	public	private
private	protected	private
private	private	not accessible

Private inheritance is similar to embedding the class inside the derived class; it's very much like a HasA relationship. You can override protected members of the base class in the derived class even when it's privately inherited. This lets you hide the implementation. You can inherit from an abstract base class and inherit the implementation privately from the base class by only exposing the interface.

In general, use public when you want to extend the capabilities of the base class and private when you want to use the capabilities of the base class but not expose them.

Caveat

Remember, if you derive privately, none of the base-class interfaces will be available outside of your class. Private inheritance is very useful, but don't overuse it.

Technique 100: Multiple Inheritance Can Cause Ambiguities

Category: Compile your code

Before

```
class C1
{
public:
   void Method1();
   void Method2();
};
```

```
class C2 : public C1
{
public:
    void Method3();
};

class C3 : public C1
{
public:
    void Method3();
};

class C4 : public C3, public C2
{
};

void TestMultInherit()
{
    C4  c4;


    //This will not compile

    c4.Method1();
    c4.Method2();
    c4.Method3();
}
```

After

```
class C1
{
public:
    void Method1();
    void Method2();
};

class C2 : public C1
{
public:
    void Method3();
};
```

```
class C3 : public C1
{
public:
   void Method3();
};

class C4 : public C3, public C2
{
};

void TestMultInherit()
{
   C4  c4;

   c4.C2::Method1();
   c4.C3::Method2();
   c4.C3::Method3();
}
```

When you have multiple inheritance, if two (or more) base classes have members with the same name or if two (or more) bases have a base class in common, you will end up in a situation where method names are ambiguous. For example, consider the "Before" code for this technique. What does c4::Method1() mean? Well, it could be the Method1 that C4 inherits from C3 that inherits from C1. Or it could be the Method1 that C4 inherits from C2 that inherits from C1.

Even if you inherit one of the classes privately, and as a result the method is not accessible, the method name will still be ambiguous.

To get around this problem, you need to state explicitly which class the method you're calling is from, as shown in the "After" code.

See example: TestMultInherit() in inherit.cpp

CHAPTER 10

Operator Overloading

OPERATOR OVERLOADING IS A VERY POWERFUL TECHNIQUE. It can help you increase code readability. At the same time, there can be very powerful side effects, some good and some bad.

Technique 101: The Difference between Pre- and Postfix Operators

Category: Compile your code

Source

```
T*operator++(void)  //Prefix
{
    return (T *)PvAt(++m_it);
}
T*operator++(int)  //Postfix
{
    return (T *)PvAt(m_it++);
}
```

Unlike other operators, the increment (++) and decrement (−−) operators can be applied as both postfix and prefix operators. When you overload these operators, you can overload the prefix case, the postfix case, or both. In general, if you overload one, you should overload the other, so as to avoid confusion.

The first format in the "Source" code for this technique provides the prefix overload; the second provides the postfix overload. Note that the (int) parameter for the postfix operator is never used.

See example: operator ++ in drg.h

Technique 102: Be Careful When You Overload Operators

Category: Avoid unexpected results

Operators are powerful. Because they are built into the language, programmers often expect them to behave in a certain way. Once you have overloaded them, however, they can behave in many different ways. This can lead to confusion and error. So overload them if you need to, but be careful.

Technique 103: Don't Change the Meaning of Operators

Category: Avoid unexpected results

Operators are defined for all of the intrinsic types, which leads programmers to have expectations as to what a particular operator means. When you overload an operator, have it act in a natural way for the particular operator. In other words, just as you wouldn't (well, shouldn't) create a member function called Print() that, instead of printing, deletes all files on the hard drive, you shouldn't overload ! = and have it do an = = or some other contradictory operation.

Technique 104: Overload = If You Expect to Use Assignment with Classes

Category: Compile your code

Before

```
class String
{
private:
    int m_cch;
    char *m_pch;
    void ReinitString(const char *pch, int cch);
public:
    String(void) : m_cch(0)
    {
        m_pch = NULL;
    }

    ~String(void)
    {
        if(m_pch)
            delete m_pch;
    }

};
```

```
void TestStringClass(void)
{
    String string1;

    string1 = "Test1";
    string1 += "Hello";
}
```

After

```
class String
{
private:
    int m_cch;
    char *m_pch;
    void ReinitString(const char *pch, int cch);
public:
    String(void) : m_cch(0)
    {
        m_pch = NULL;
    }

    ~String(void)
    {
        if(m_pch)
            delete m_pch;
    }

    const String& operator=(const String &string)
    {
        if(&string != this)
            ReinitString(string.m_pch, string.m_cch);
        return *this;
    }

    const String& operator=(const char *sz)
    {
        ReinitString(sz, strlen(sz));
        return *this;
    }

};
```

```
void TestStringClass(void)
{
    String string1;

    string1 = "Test1";
    string1 += "Hello";
}
```

It is natural to want to use = to initialize the value of some object, as you can see in the "Before" code for this technique. The = operator works with intrinsic types, such as float and int. If you want it to work with a class that you've created, you will need to overload the = operator, as shown in the "After" code.

Note that, in the absence of an overloaded = operator, the compiler will simply do a memcpy. If the class has pointers to allocated data, you may experience problems because both the source and copy instance would have pointers to the same data. If one instance deletes the data, the other still has a reference. That's just a problem waiting to happen.

Caveat

When you overload an operator, the operator will work when the class is the left operand. That is because the left operand determines the object to which the operator belongs. This is the same as a function. The function pfoo->Bar() expects the Bar function to be a member of the Foo class. For example, with the String class you can do the following:

```
string1 = "Test1";
```

However, you can't do the following with the String class because the = operator for char * can't take String as a parameter:

```
char *foo;
foo = string1;
```

See example: class String in string.cpp

Technique 105: Operators Can Do More Work than You Think

Category: Write faster code

Source

```
class String
{
private:
    int m_cch;
    char *m_pch;
public:

    int operator==(const String& string) const
    {
        return(strcmp(m_pch, string.m_pch) == 0);
    }
    int operator==(const char *sz) const
    {
        return(strcmp(m_pch, sz) == 0);
    }

    int operator>(const String& string) const
    {
        return(strcmp(m_pch, string.m_pch) > 0);
    }
    int operator>(const char *sz) const
    {
        return(strcmp(m_pch, sz) > 0);
    }
    int operator<(const String& string) const
    {
        return(strcmp(m_pch, string.m_pch) < 0);
    }
    int operator<(const char *sz) const
    {
        return(strcmp(m_pch, sz) < 0);
    }
};
```

```
void TestStringClass(void)
{
    String string("Test");
    String string1(string);

    if(string1 == string)
        string1 = "equal";
    else if(string1 < string)
        string1 = "less";
    else
        string1 = "greater";
}
```

Operators let you write code that is succinct and easy to understand. But that doesn't mean that the result is fast and efficient. For example, consider the "Source" example shown for this technique. The TestStringClass() function compares two strings to see whether one string is equal to, greater than, or less than the other. Looking at the operator code, you can see that == calls strcmp to see if the two strings are equal. Likewise, < calls strcmp to see if one string is less than the other. Thus, if the strings are not equal, strcmp gets called twice (once for the == check and once for the < check).

What's the problem? Well, strcmp returns either zero, a negative, or a positive number to indicate how two strings compare. Thus, you can determine how string1 and string compare with a single call to strcmp rather than two calls. The operator code is easy to read but not as efficient as you could write it.

See example: TestStringClass() in string.cpp

Technique 106: Don't Return References to Local Variables

Category: Avoid crashes and unexpected results

Before

```
String &operator+(const String&string) const
    {
        String stringNew(m_pch);

        stringNew.Append(string.m_pch, string.m_cch);
        return stringNew;
    }
```

After

```
String operator+(const String&string) const
    {
        String stringNew(m_pch);

        stringNew.Append(string.m_pch, string.m_cch);
        return stringNew;
    }
```

Notice the subtle difference between the "Before" and "After" code for this technique. The operator in the "Before" code returns a reference to a String. The operator in the "After" code returns a copy of a String.

Because stringNew is allocated on the stack, the operator in the "Before" code is returning a reference to a stack-based variable. The variable will be destroyed after the operator loses scope. This will lead either to bad data or to a crash. When you compile the code, you will get a warning. Pay attention to that warning.

By contrast, the "After" code returns a copy of the variable rather than a reference to the variable, and the problem is averted.

See example: String operator+ in string.cpp

See also: Technique 53

Templates

HEY, WE'VE GONE ALL OUT IN THIS CHAPTER to discuss template techniques. Okay, we only have one technique here, but it's a really good one.

Technique 107: Keep the Template Implementation in a Different Class

Category: Write more efficient code

Before

```
template <class T>
class Drg
{
private:
   int m_it;
   T  PvAppend(T* pv, long lcItem=1);
   T  PvAt(long lindex) const;
public:
   Drg() : m_it(0)
   {
   }
   Drg(const Drg<T> &drg)
   {
      m_it = drg.m_it;
   }

   T &operator*(void) const
   {
      return *(T *)PvAt(m_it);
   }

   T *Append(const T &t)
   {
      return (T *)PvAppend((void *)&t);
   }
};
```

After

```
class Drgbase
{
private:
    BYTE *  m_pbMac;
public:
    void *  PvAppend(void * pv, long lcItem=1);
    void *  PvAt(long lindex) const;
};


template <class T>
class Drg : private Drgbase
{
private:
    int m_it;
public:
    Drg() : Drgbase(sizeof(T)), m_it(0)
    {
    }
    Drg(const Drg<T> &drg) : Drgbase(drg)
    {
        m_it = drg.m_it;
    }

    T &operator*(void) const
    {
        return *(T *)PvAt(m_it);
    }

    T *Append(const T &t)
    {
        return (T *)PvAppend((void *)&t);
    }
};
```

When you use templates, each instantiation of the template contains all of the code from the template declaration. For example, suppose you were to create a Drg<char>, Drg<int> and Drg<foo>. With the "Before" code shown for this technique, each one of these implementations would have a copy of PvAppend, PvAt, and any other helper functions. Of course, each of these functions would be customized for the particular data type in use.

By contrast, consider the "After" code. Here, we've created a base class called Drgbase. In it, we create a set of helper functions that operate on void pointers (void *). The templatized class inherits from this class. Its public members provide type-safe access to the helper functions. Unlike the "Before" code, however, each instance of the templatized class in the new code doesn't duplicate all of the helper functions. Rather, each instance just uses the common base-class implementations, reducing code size and thus leading to faster code.

See example: class Drgbase and Drg in drg.h

CHAPTER 12

Miscellaneous Goop

THIS CHAPTER IS A BIT OF A CATCHALL. We discuss a variety of techniques, from working around compiler oddities to methods for keeping objects from being created on the stack. The only theme in common is that none of these techniques fit in the other chapters.

Technique 108: Inserting Graphic File Resources

Category: Workaround

If you want to include JPEG, GIF, or other non-BMP graphics inside of an RC file you may need to use this technique. Follow these steps:

1. Change the file extension to an unknown type, for example from JPG to FOO.

2. Click on Insert → Resource.

3. Click on the Import button.

4. Change the Files of type drop down to show all files.

5. Double click on the file you want to import.

6. Type in data as the resource type.

When you import a graphic file as a custom resource, Visual C++ automatically converts the graphics to BMP format. Why? Who knows. BMP files are the only types of graphic files with built-in Windows support. So maybe it thinks it is doing you a favor. But BMP files take up significantly more memory than JPGs and GIFs. And if you are expecting a JPEG and instead find a BMP, you won't be able to read the file. Because Visual C++ checks the file extension to determine whether to convert the file, this workaround will fool it.

Technique 109: Make Sure Your Paths Are Correct

Category: Avoid hard-to-find problems

Making sure your paths are correct is a technique to use when you use libraries or header files other than those supplied with the compiler.

Follow these steps:

1. Select Tools → Options.

2. Click on the Directories tab.

3. Select the Include files drop down.

4. Check out the order in which directories are searched.

5. Select the Library files drop down.

6. Check out the order in which directories are searched.

The order in which directories appear in this dialog is the order in which they will be searched. If you add new components to your system, they will sometimes install libraries or header files that are meant to replace those that come with the compiler. If you don't make sure that such replacement libraries are found before the compiler libraries are, you may end up with a mismatch. For example, if you install the DirectX SDK, it will provide header files and libraries that replace several of the multimedia-related libraries and headers. Be sure that the paths to the DirectX libraries and headers occur before those for the compiler's libraries and headers.

Also be sure that your header and library file paths are in synch. For example, suppose you install the DirectX SDK. Make sure you update the path for both the header files and the libraries. If you don't, you can easily end up with a situation where your program compiles and links but doesn't do the right thing.

Technique 110: Keep Reference-Counted Objects off the Stack

Category: Avoid crashes and unexpected results

Before

```
class RefCounted
{
```

```
public:
    RefCounted()
    {
    }

    ~RefCounted()
    {
    }
}
```

After

```
class RefCounted
{
public:
    RefCounted()
    {
    }
private:
    ~RefCounted()
    {
    }
}
```

When you create reference-counted objects, you need to make sure that the reference counts are properly updated. This means that you need to increment the count before using the object and then decrement it once you are finished.

The object itself controls its lifetime. Therefore, you can't delete the object. Rather, the method that decrements the use counter (such as Release in the Ref-Counted class) is in charge of deleting the object. When the use count goes to zero, the method deletes the object.

Because of this, you need to prevent the object from being created on the stack. In other words, you don't want the programmer to be able to write code such as the following:

```
RefCounted foo;
```

Why not? Because this code will create an object on the stack. When the function ends, the object will be automatically deleted, overriding any reference counting. (Also, objects created on the stack disappear when the function ends, so they can't be used outside of the function scope, as discussed in Technique 53.)

Making the destructor private, as shown in the "After" code for this technique, does the trick. If the compiler can't find a public destructor, it won't let you create the object on the stack.

See example: class RefCounted in access.cpp

Technique 111: Passing Preallocated Memory to new

Category: Write faster code

Source

```
class DemoOfNew
{
private:
    int m_i;
    void *operator new(size_t cbAlloc)
    {
        // Should never be called.
        return NULL;
    }
public:
    void *operator new(size_t cbAlloc, void *pv)
    {
        return pv;
    }
    void operator delete(void * pv)
    {
    }
    DemoOfNew():m_i(0)
    {
        cout << "DemoOfNew Ctor called\n";
    }
    ~DemoOfNew()
    {
        cout << "DemoOfNew Dtor called\n";
    }
    void SetI(int i)
    {
        m_i = i;
    }
```

```
    int GetI(void)
    {
        return m_i;
    }
};
void TestMemAllocatorNew()
{

    void *pv;
    DemoOfNew *pdemoofnew;

    pv = malloc(sizeof(DemoOfNew));

    pdemoofnew = new (pv) DemoOfNew;
    pdemoofnew->SetI(10);
    cout <<pdemoofnew->GetI() << '\n';
    delete pdemoofnew;
    free(pv);
}
```

For performance reasons, it can be useful to preallocate memory for classes. For example, you may want to perform the memory allocations during start-up or before a performance-critical section of code executes.

There are two steps to using preallocated memory: (1) allocating memory of the correct size and (2) then overriding the new operator to use the preallocated memory. In this technique's "Source" code, you can see that the DemoOfNew class overrides new to disable it. It also has a version of new that takes the preallocated memory and returns a pointer to that memory. The compiler will generate the code for automatically calling the constructor on this memory. The TestMemAllocatorNew function allocates memory and then passes the preallocated memory to the new call for DemoOfNew as follows:

```
pdemoofnew = new (pv) DemoOfNew;
```

Note that, even though delete appears not to do anything, it forces the compiler to generate the call to the destructor.

Caveat

This is an advanced technique that can land you in trouble if you don't know exactly what you are doing. You are better off shipping code that works than you are shipping clever, fast code that doesn't work.

Technique 112: Aliasing with References

Category: Avoid stupid mistakes

Before

```
void TestAliasing(long &la, long &lb)
{
   la = 10;
   lb = 20;
}
```

After

```
void TestAliasing(long &la, long &lb)
{
   if(&la == &lb)
      la = 20;
   else
   {
      la = 10;
      lb = 20;
   }
}
```

In the "Before" code for this technique, we set the values of two variables passed in by reference. But what happens if the user passes in the same variable for both parameters? In that case, both la and lb will be references to the same variable.

Sometimes it is okay to have two references to the same variable. In other cases, you could have all types of unexpected results. At the very least, you need to be aware of and plan for the possibility. In the "After" code here, we check for aliasing before we assign values to the variables.

See example: TestAliasing() in misc.cpp

See also: Technique 55

CHAPTER 13

Performance

WHO SAYS SIZE DOESN'T MATTER? When it comes to performance, it certainly does. The bigger your code, the slower it usually is. This is especially true with the new Pentium hardware, where there is a limited cache—and the performance cost of finding your code and data in the cache makes all the difference between speedy and sluggish. If it's not in the primary or secondary cache, the processor needs to fetch the data or code from the main memory. This means that the processor will spend more cycles in the fetch than it will in executing instructions. This chapter is filled with techniques to help you improve your code's performance.

Technique 113: Design Is More Important than Tuning

Category: Advice

No matter how good you are at tweaking code to get the best performance out of it, you can't make a bad design go fast. Using better data structures and algorithms will give far better performance gains than any amount of tuning can. For example, it used to be that PC file systems kept the directory file names in an array. Finding a particular file meant searching through the linear list. The more files you had in the directory, the slower access would become. Tuning the code didn't have nearly the same impact as switching to a btree. All of a sudden, with the btree, file access became much faster.

Understand the typical customer usage. Understand the problem bounds. Think about the approach you have taken to the problem and the assumptions you made. Then think about better approaches. Question your infrastructure. Did you really need a garbage collector? Do you need to have transaction support for everything? Did you end up with more data than you thought and your time is spent finding data linearly? Did you design for huge sets of data but actually have small sets, so that simpler approaches might work better?

For example, we were once working on a query language that had a construct for finding the nth record in a database. It turned out that the most frequent queries were for finding the first and last records. By changing the structures and special casing those queries, we achieved dramatic speed gains.

Quite often, one can more easily make simpler designs work faster because they are easier to understand and change.

Technique 114: Know What to Improve

Category: Advice

Profile your code and see where time is spent. You may think that all of your time is spent tokenizing but then find out that ninety percent of your time is spent copying strings. If so, making the tokenizer ten times faster won't have nearly the impact as will reducing the time spent copying strings. Many times the slow downs aren't where you expect.

There are several third-party profilers on the market. Consider buying one.

Technique 115: Instrument Your Code

Category: Write faster code

Source

```
clocktStart = clock();
for(j =0;j<1000;j++)
{
    for(int i=0;i<g_cDegrees;i++)
    {
        dblT += trig.DblSineLUT(i);
        dblT += trig.DblCosineLUT(i);
    }
}
clocktFinish = clock();
cout << dblT << '\n';
```

Use profiling when you want to determine where the bottlenecks in your code are and where time is generally being spent. Use instrumentation when you want to compare a few techniques in order to determine which is the fastest approach.

Perform your timing over a large sample, such as 1,000 or 100,000 repetitions, so that overhead and burps will be averaged out and the results will be more stable. Have the time value large enough that it can be measured in milliseconds (or some larger time value).

Caveat

Make sure that you are comparing apples to apples. For example, working with benchmarking in the "Before" code in Technique 126 in this chapter, we initially coded the nonintrinsic to be through a call and the intrinsic directly in line. This unfavorably added call overhead to the nonintrinsic approach and skewed the results.

See example: `TestTrig()` in misc.cpp

Technique 116: Reduce Your Working Set

Category: Advice

With modern processors, reducing secondary cache hits and out-of-cache hits is often more important than anything else when it comes to performance tuning. Thus, reducing the working set of your code is key. Find out what is chewing memory. Understand the libraries you use. Don't load DLLs that you don't need to. Reduce the size of elements in your data structures. Don't keep garbage around that you don't need. Eliminate bloat.

In general, data takes up more space than the code. Code usually has a known cost. Data is unknown. So when you are trying to reduce the working set, focus on reducing both code size and data size. Take care that you don't concentrate solely on reducing the code size and ignore the working set increase caused by having redundant pointers or other wasteful data structure elements. Above all, use profilers and instrument your executable to discover working set and performance problems.

Technique 117: Use the optimize for space Flag

Category: Write faster code

Choosing the `Minimize size` optimization not only makes your code smaller but also, because it reduces working set, makes your code faster. In general, when you go to release your code, choose the `Minimize size` option. (Use the /O1 flag when using command line tools.)

Of course, be sure to measure your performance before and after your optimizations. Don't assume that they will perform magic for you. Watch out for the "I have a hammer, so everything is a nail" syndrome.

Technique 118: Delay Loading

Category: Write faster code

The less junk you have in memory, the faster your code will run and load. If you load all of your DLLs when the program starts, you'll have slow start-up time. If there are certain DLLs that you only use in certain circumstances, load them when those circumstances arise. Your program will start and execute faster.

Caveat

DLLs are expensive to load. They also need to go through fix ups. If you delay load too many DLLs, you'll find awkward stutters as they load and are initialized. Reduce the number of DLLs that the program has to use. Combine them together if you can. Also, don't forget to set the base address of the DLL. This will tell the loader that it should always try to load your DLL at a particular address. In turn, the DLLs used by your program will not be competing for one address space.

Check out the REBASE command line tool in the Microsoft Platform SDK, and make it part of your build process. It takes a collection of EXE/DLLs and re-bases them to avoid base address collisions.

Technique 119: Invest in Good Tools

Category: Advice

Performance tuning can be difficult, so make sure you have a good profiler. There are also excellent tools for analyzing code usage during typical executions. These can provide all sorts of hints for making your code more efficient.

Technique 120: Templates Usually Mean Bloat

Category: Advice

Although templates can make your code cleaner looking, they often introduce a lot of code bloat. Be very careful when you use them.

Likewise, be careful when you use macros and inline functions because these can expand your code size as well.

See also: Technique 107

Technique 121: Floating Point Is Faster than Integer Math on a Pentium

Category: Write faster code

Before the Pentium chip, with its built-in floating-point processor, it used to be much faster to do integer arithmetic than floating-point arithmetic. As a result, many of us would figure out clever ways to recast problems as integer problems.

With the Pentium, it is the other way around: floating-point math is faster than integer math. So don't go to great lengths to convert floating-point calculations to integer calculations. Your code will be slower. Instead, you will be better off actually going in the reverse.

Caveat

Floating-point numbers take up more space than integers. Depending on your application, you may find storage size more important than raw processing speed.

As always, measure and profile your code to determine the best approach. Don't assume that a technique we suggest will always work for all situations. Be sure to verify before you deploy.

Technique 122: Look-Up Tables Can Increase Performance

Category: Write faster code

Source

```
const int g_cDegrees = 900;
class Trig
{
private:
    double m_rgdblSin[g_cDegrees];
    double m_rgdblCos[g_cDegrees];
public:
    Trig()
    {
        int idbl;
        double dbl;
        double dblPIBy4=atan(1.0);
        double dblPIBy2=dblPIBy4 * 2.0;
```

```
            // 1/10th of a degree in radians.
        double dbl10thDegToRad=dblPIBy4/450;

        for(idbl=0, dbl=0.0; dbl<dblPIBy2; dbl+= dbl10thDegToRad, idbl++)
        {
            m_rgdblSin[idbl] = sin(dbl);
            m_rgdblCos[idbl] = cos(dbl);
        }
    }
    double DblSineLUT(int iDeg);
    double DblCosineLUT(int iDeg);
    double DblSine(double dblAngle);
    double DblCosine(double dblAngle);
    double DblSineIntrinsic(double dblAngle);
    double DblCosineIntrinsic(double dblAngle);
};

double Trig::DblSineLUT(int iDeg)
{
    if(iDeg >= g_cDegrees || iDeg < 0)
        return 0.0;
    return m_rgdblSin[iDeg];
}

double Trig::DblCosineLUT(int iDeg)
{
    if(iDeg >= g_cDegrees || iDeg < 0)
        return 0.0;
    return m_rgdblCos[iDeg];
}

double Trig::DblSine(double dblAngle)
{
    return sin(dblAngle);
}

double Trig::DblCosine(double dblAngle)
{
    return cos(dblAngle);
}

#pragma intrinsic(sin, cos)
double Trig::DblSineIntrinsic(double dblAngle)
```

```
{
    return sin(dblAngle);
}
double Trig::DblCosineIntrinsic(double dblAngle)
{
    return cos(dblAngle);
}
```

Some calculations take a long time to compute. For example, even though the Pentium has built-in instructions for trigonometric functions, they take a while to execute. Custom algorithms can take even longer.

If execution speed is more important than accuracy, consider using a look-up table. With a look-up table, you fill an array with precomputed results for a variety of values. When you need to find the result for a particular value, you find the index in the array nearest to that value.

For example, suppose you want to create a look-up table for sin. Because you know that sin is cyclic, you only need to find values for the range from 0 to 2π. Let's say that you decide to make the array 100 elements long. You would initialize the array by filling it with the values of sin starting with 0 radians and incrementing by $2\pi/100$ radians. When you want to find the value of sin for a particular angle, you would then find the closest angle in the look-up table.

In the "Source" code shown for this technique, we've created a look-up table for calculating sin and cos values. We also have functions that determine the value using the CRT sin and cos functions and intrinsic sin and cos functions.

The look-up table is clearly the winner. Table 13.1 shows the results for finding the sin and cos of 900,000 values on the PII-300 with which we tested the code.

Table 13.1   Timings for Look-Up Table Performance Tests

Technique	Time
Look-up table	.07 seconds
Trigonometric functions	.931 seconds
Intrinsic trigonometric functions	.751 seconds

Caveat

Note that, depending on what you do, the speed of determining the index within the look-up table can outweigh the advantage of using the look-up table. Benchmark your code. If you can store your units internally in terms of the look-up table size—and thus avoid conversions during the look up—you'll have far faster code.

Also note that the amount of error in the look-up table is a function of the expression used for calculating the table as well as the number of entries. Some functions have rapid growth near certain values. For example, sin grows quickly near 0 degrees. You will have more error in the look-up table for angles close to 0 degrees than you will for angles close to 90 degrees.

Finally, note that this type of optimization is heavily dependent on the processor. If the processor has a built-in function for what you are doing, it may quite possibly be faster than using a look-up table. Benchmark your code to make sure that your look-up table is faster.

See example: Class Trig in misc.cpp

Technique 123: Be Cautious When Using Inline Functions

Category: Advice

Inline functions can make your code faster because they avoid function call overhead. But inline functions also make your code larger because they place the function body directly within your code. In general, having smaller code increases your performance far more than does reducing the function call overhead. Thus, you are usually better off if you use inline functions sparingly.

Technique 124: Know What Code Is Generated

Category: Write faster code

Source

```
int main(int argc, char* argv[])
{
    unsigned long a, b;
    long sA, sB;

    b = 17;
    sB = 17;

    a = b / 32;
    sA = sB / 32;
    sA = sB >> 5;

/*
    27:        a = b / 32;
    0040ED86    mov         eax,dword ptr [ebp-8]
```

```
    0040ED89    shr            eax,5
    0040ED8C    mov            dword ptr [ebp-4],eax
    28:         sA = sB / 32;
    0040ED8F    mov            eax,dword ptr [ebp-10h]
    0040ED92    cdq
    0040ED93    and            edx,1Fh
    0040ED96    add            eax,edx
    0040ED98    sar            eax,5
    0040ED9B    mov            dword ptr [ebp-0Ch],eax
    29:         sA = sB >> 5;
    0040ED9E    mov            ecx,dword ptr [ebp-10h]
    0040EDA1    sar            ecx,5
    0040EDA4    mov            dword ptr [ebp-0Ch],ecx
*/

    return 0;
}
```

The code that gets generated by the compiler may not be what you expect. For example, consider the line a = b/32 in the "Source" code for this technique. Looking at the assembly language generated (which here we have compiled with optimization set to minimize space), you can see that the compiler is using a shr. (This is, of course, far faster than a div.)

If, however, we used signed rather than unsigned numbers, as is shown by the line sA = sB/32, the compiler adds a bunch of code to do sign fix ups. If we instead use a >> operator, far-faster code is generated. Thus, you can see that, if you have signed variables, such as longs, but you know a value is positive, you are far better off doing a shift than a divide.

The moral of the story is, don't assume you know what is generated by the compiler. Take a look at the code. The way you write your expressions can make a big difference in how the code gets generated.

Technique 125: Shifts Are Faster than Divides

Category: Write faster code

Before

```
long sA, sB;

sB = 17;
sA = sB / 32;
```

After

```
long sA, sB;

sB = 17;
sA = sB >> 5;
```

The >> and << operators are far faster than divides. If you are dividing by powers of two, you can use the shift operators instead of a divide. Note, of course, that this only applies to integers.

Caveat

It is usually harder to read shifts than it is to read divides and multiplies. If you are doing unsigned arithmetic and dividing by constants, the compiler will generate shifts instead of a divide for you, as shown in the previous technique. So, don't overuse this technique.

Also, remember that A/2 is not the same as A >> 2. (A/2 is the same as A >> 1.)

Technique 126: Pointer Arithmetic Is Not Faster than Array Look Ups

Category: Write cleaner code

Before

```
void TestBuff()
{
    char rgch[256];
    int ich;

    ich = 0;
    while(ich < sizeof(rgch))
        rgch[ich++] = ' ';
    rgch[sizeof(rgch)-1] = 0;
    cout << rgch << '\n';
}
```

After

```
void TestBuff()
{
    char rgch[256];
    char *pch;
    char *pchMac;

    pch = rgch;
    pchMac = rgch+sizeof(rgch)-1;
    while(pch < pchMac)
        *pch++ = 't';
    rgch[sizeof(rgch)-1] = 0;
    cout << rgch << '\n';
}
```

Conventional programming wisdom states that using pointer arithmetic is faster than using array indexing and that it is therefore worth writing the harder-to-read pointer-based code. Well, with today's compilers, this isn't really true. Writing array code will, for the most part, give you the same performance as writing pointer-based code. Of course, pointer-based code will look studlier.

Let's take a look at the assembly generated by the heart of the loop in the "Before" code for this technique:

```
11:             rgch[ich++] = ' ';
0040103F    mov         eax,dword ptr [ich]
00401045    mov         byte ptr rgch[eax],20h
0040104D    mov         ecx,dword ptr [ich]
00401053    add         ecx,1
00401056    mov         dword ptr [ich],ecx
```

Now, compare that to the code generated by the heart of the loop in the "After" code:

```
17:             *pch++ = 't';
00401099    mov         eax,dword ptr [pch]
0040109C    mov         byte ptr [eax],74h
0040109F    mov         ecx,dword ptr [pch]
004010A2    add         ecx,1
004010A5    mov         dword ptr [pch],ecx
```

Hmm, not much difference.

For this case, you'd be better off using the easier-to-read array code. In short, conventional wisdom isn't always correct. When in doubt, check out the actual code generated.

See example: TestBuff() in misc.cpp

Technique 127: Memory Allocations Are Expensive

Category: Write faster code

Before

```
if(m_pstream)
    delete m_pstream;
m_pstream = (PSTREAM)new FILESTREAM(TRUE);
```

After

```
if(m_pstream)
{
    if(m_pstream->GetStreamType() != streamtypeFile)
    {
        delete m_pstream;
        m_pstream = NULL;
    }
}
if(NULL == m_pstream)
    m_pstream = (PSTREAM)new FILESTREAM(TRUE);
```

Allocating memory and creating handles (such as file handles, memory handles, stream handles, etc.) is expensive. Deleting memory is often even more expensive because memory managers often delay cleanup of data structures until deletes occur. Avoid allocating and deleting memory and handles when possible. For example, the "Before" code for this technique deletes an existing handle and creates a new one, whereas the "After" code checks whether the handle is a file handle. If so, it reuses it.

In addition to being wary of how your code allocates memory, you may also want to write your own memory allocator. If you know the way that you will use memory, you can gain significant speed over the generic system memory managers. Do so, however, only with great caution and only if you know exactly what you are doing. When in doubt, just use the standard memory allocators. Although creating your own memory manager can be faster, it can also introduce a lot of unpleasant bugs.

Technique 128: Be Careful When Using String Functions

Category: Write faster code

Before

```
//m_pch is m_cch characters long
strcpy(pchNew, m_pch);
strcat(pchNew, pch);
```

After

```
//m_pch is m_cch characters long
strcpy(pchNew, m_pch);
strcpy(pchNew+m_cch, pch);
```

Really, this technique applies to any function. Knowing how a function works can help you operate more efficiently. This is particularly true with string functions, which have a habit of walking through the string looking for the ending null.

For example, consider the "Before" code for this technique. Here, we are concatenating two strings together. The code looks innocent enough. But `strcat` walks the entire destination string to find the end before concatenating in the source string. Because we already know the length of the string (at least in this example), walking through the whole destination string wastes time. The "After" code avoids this completely by using pointer arithmetic to jump to the end of the string. It then does a `strcpy`.

See example: `String::Append()` in string.cpp

Technique 129: Avoid the CRT If You Can

Category: Write faster code

The C Runtime (CRT) is a library of common functions used by most programs. It includes start-up code as well as many other functions. It also adds a lot of space to your programs. When you focus on size, you can write your own start-up code and reproduce only the CRT functions you need, thus dramatically lowering the size of your programs.

Technique 130: Intrinsics Are Faster than the CRT

Category: Write faster code

Source

```
#pragma intrinsic(sin, cos)
double Trig::DblSineIntrinsic(double dblAngle)
{
    return sin(dblAngle);
}
```

The Pentium chip has a lot of powerful functions built directly into the hardware. For example, it has various trigonometric functions available as floating-point assembly instructions.

The CRT has software versions of these functions for machines that don't have floating-point processors.

It is faster to call the intrinsic functions directly, although this will generate code that can only work on certain classes of machines, such as Pentiums and later models. Using intrinsics also reduces your code size because you don't link in a bunch of goop from the CRT (although depending on what you call, you could end up with more inline code than you would like).

You can turn on intrinsics with the #pragma command as shown in this section's "Source" code. You can also turn them on globally from Visual Studio by using the following steps:

1. Select Project → Settings.

2. Click on the C++ tab.

3. Select Optimizations from the Category drop down.

4. Check on Generate Intrinsic Functions.

From the command line, specify the /Oi flag.
See example: `Trig::DblSineIntrinsic()` in misc.cpp

CHAPTER 14

Using Assembly

IF YOU WANT ULTIMATE CONTROL OVER YOUR CODE or need to do some very tight optimizations on frequently called code, you may want to incorporate assembly language into your program. This chapter includes a few techniques for doing so.

Technique 131: C++ Variables Can Be Directly Accessed from Assembly

Category: Avoid unexpected results

Source

```
#pragma warning( disable : 4035 )
int RExp::IChInSz(unsigned char chSrc, const char *pch, int cch)
{
_asm
    {
    xor eax, eax
    mov al, chSrc
    mov edi, pch
    mov ecx, cch
    cld
    repnz scasb
    jz Found
    xor eax, eax
    jmp End
Found:
    mov eax, cch
    sub eax, ecx
End:
    dec eax
    }
}
#pragma warning( default : 4035 )
```

   C++ variables can be directly accessed in assembly language, as is done in
this technique's "Source" sample with the chSrc parameter. Doing so makes it very

easy to mix assembly with C++ code. Be sure, however, that you don't use variable names that clash with reserved assembly names. For example, it would be a bad idea to have a C++ variable named eax. The assembler will treat that as a reference to the eax register, not to the C++ variable. Likewise, avoid names such as PUSH, sub, repnz, and so forth. They will all get you into trouble.

Technique 132: Use Inline Assembly Only If You Are Writing for a Specific Processor

Category: Compile your code

Assembly code is not portable code. Assembly code written for the Pentium will not work on an Alpha chip. Code written specifically for MMX processors will not work on machines that don't have MMX support.

To add assembly to your code, use _asm followed by {}, as follows:

```
_asm
   {
   xor eax, eax
   mov al, chSrc
   }
```

Technique 133: You Don't Need to Use return If eax Is Already Set

Category: Write cleaner code

Source

```
#pragma warning( disable : 4035 )
int RExp::IChInSz(unsigned char chSrc, const char *pch, int cch)
{
_asm
   {
   xor eax, eax
   mov al, chSrc
   mov edi, pch
   mov ecx, cch
   cld
   repnz scasb
   jz Found
   xor eax, eax
   jmp End
```

```
Found:
    mov eax, cch
    sub eax, ecx
End:
    dec eax
    }
}
#pragma warning( default : 4035 )
```

The return value from a function is placed in eax. If your assembly code already fills eax with the desired value, you don't need to end your function with a return. In fact, setting eax from within the assembly code is a nice way to return a value from the function because you don't need to go through any extra steps after the assembly code ends.

Technique 134: If You Set eax from Assembly, Disable Warning 4035

Category: Compile your code

Source

```
#pragma warning( disable : 4035 )
int RExp::IChInSz(unsigned char chSrc, const char *pch, int cch)
{
_asm
    {
    xor eax, eax
    mov al, chSrc
    mov edi, pch
    mov ecx, cch
    cld
    repnz scasb
    jz Found
    xor eax, eax
    jmp End
Found:
    mov eax, cch
    sub eax, ecx
End:
    dec eax
    }
}
#pragma warning( default : 4035 )
```

If you set eax in your assembly code, and thus don't have a return statement, you'll get a warning. To avoid this warning, disable warning 4035 as shown in the code here.

Make sure that you set this pragma outside of the function.

Technique 135: Always Restore Warning Defaults after You Disable Them

Category: Avoid unexpected results

Source

```
#pragma warning( disable : 4035 )
int RExp::IChInSz(unsigned char chSrc, const char *pch, int cch)
{
_asm
    {
    xor eax, eax
    mov al, chSrc
    mov edi, pch
    mov ecx, cch
    cld
    repnz scasb
    jz Found
    xor eax, eax
    jmp End
Found:
    mov eax, cch
    sub eax, ecx
End:
    dec eax
    }
}
#pragma warning( default : 4035 )
```

If you disable a warning, as is done in this technique's "Source" code for the missing return statement warning, be sure that you return the warning to its default setting after you are finished with your assembly code. If you don't, you won't get that warning for the rest of the file. And that could be bad news if you have mistakes in your code.

CHAPTER 15
General Debugging Stuff

IN THIS CHAPTER, WE GO OVER SOME GENERAL ADVICE and approaches to debugging. Then in the next chapter, we'll walk through some specific debugging techniques.

Technique 136: What's a Bug?

Category: Advice

What *is* a bug? Some stupid mistake? A careless oversight? A bug is the difference between what you think the code is doing and what the code actually is doing. It's really tempting to go through your code quickly when you're debugging, examining only where you think the problem is. Sometimes you'll be right. But you're usually much better off going through the code slowly and seeing what it actually does.

Technique 137: Debug Your Design before You Code

Category: Advice

It's tempting to come up with a design and jump right in and code. Heck, that's the fun part. And, after all, the deadline's approaching.

Be patient. It's always better to work through your design and look for problems before you begin coding. Ask yourself: Does it solve the right problem? Does it deal with edge conditions? Is it overly complex? What issues are going to show up? Is there a better approach?

Walk through your design with some sample data and see if it does what you expect. Show it to a coworker. Do a design review. Prototype, and then fix your design based on what you discover as you prototype. Only then should you start your real code. In short, fix your design before you code.

Technique 138: Always Single Step through New Code

Category: Avoid stupid mistakes

It's easy to assume that your code works. After all, you're a pro—of course you programmed what you were supposed to.

Wrong. Single stepping through new code is one of the most important techniques you can follow when it comes to debugging. The best programmers do it; the ones who know enough to be dangerous don't.

After you write a piece of new code, single step through it, no matter how trivial it is. Carefully think through what each action does. Are you setting the variables you think you are? Are you going through loops the way you think you are? Have you initialized everything you need to? Are you calculating what you wanted to? Are you storing the results where you think you are? Are you getting the results you expect?

Don't do this by looking over the code. Do it in the debugger. Watch both the data and the code. The debugger will force you to see the difference between what you think the code is doing and what it actually is doing.

Technique 139: Debug If You Can, Build If You Must

Category: Advice

This is another technique that is really important but tempting to ignore.

When you have a problem with your code, figure out what is going wrong. Step through it in the debugger. Understand the issues. Don't immediately start trying fixes for what you think the problem might be. You will just end up confused and, worse, may introduce more bugs.

Likewise, if the code isn't working, avoid the temptation to chuck it and start from scratch. You may end up having to throw it all away anyway, but first understand what you did wrong. In the process, either you will discover a mistake you'll now know to not repeat or you will come up with a new and better approach to the problem.

Technique 140: Debug Data, Not Code

Category: Advice

Looking for the code that has a problem is like looking for a needle in a haystack. Looking for where data went bad is like being a detective following clues.

Bugs result in wrong data. Otherwise you'd never know about them. Don't jump in and start looking at your algorithms and execution flow. Instead, follow the data as it goes through your code. Looking at where the data gets set to a value it shouldn't will show you where your bug is.

Technique 141: Know the Code That Is Generated

Category: Advice

The product you ship is compiled code, not source code. So you need to be familiar with the actual assembly code that is generated, not just the source code. It is a good idea to debug looking at the mixed listing, not just the source listing. This way you can see exactly what is going on. Even if you don't debug in this manner, make sure you look at the actual code that is generated.

    See also: Technique 124

Technique 142: Plan for Testing

Category: Advice

Your code is going to be tested. (Or at least, we hope it will be tested.) Know it. Love it. Plan for it. Make testing easier. Here are some things you can do:

- Review your design with the test team before you begin coding.

- Think about the edge conditions.

- Create some simple tests that you will use to verify that your code works for at least the common cases. Run through those tests before you check in your code. Run through those tests every time you make a fix to your code.

- Document your code.

- Put hooks into your UI code so that it can be tested with automation software.

Technique 143: Test Early, Test Often

Category: Advice

If your code isn't thoroughly tested, your users will find your bugs. That is not only embarrassing, but it can be expensive. Find your bugs before you inflict them on others. Don't wait until the end of a cycle to begin testing. Incrementally test what you can as you develop. Some bugs will block other bugs, so the sooner you can squash bugs, the better.

Technique 144: Test under Stress Conditions

Category: Advice

Ever heard the expression "It works on my machine"? We have. We always say, "Great. Ship your machine to the customer."

Some bugs only show up in odd situations. Test with low memory. Test with low disk space. Test with slow machines. Test with net failures or slow net access. Test with lots of other applications running at the same time. Test with very large data sets. Do you use threads? Test with a multiprocessor machine. Does your code run on the server? Test with a heavy server load. Do you play media? Test without a sound card.

Technique 145: Test with Edge Conditions

Category: Advice

You should also test with conditions you may think would never occur. Delete files that are needed. Read from a bad floppy. Remove the floppy in the middle of a read. Feed your program bad data. Does it want a social security number? Give it a birthday. It wants a salary? Give it 25 billion. It wants a date? Give it 2001. (Just kidding. After all, who would ever have a problem going beyond the year 2000?)

Sounds insane? Your customer may well do these things. Fix the problems before your customers find them.

Technique 146: Test from the User's Perspective

Category: Advice

Test teams quite often write a lot of specific feature tests. These are critical for making sure that each part of the product works the way it is supposed to. But you should also test from a user's perspective. Create typical-use scenarios and test those. You may find unexpected bugs from components that don't talk to each other. Or from components that left behind trash that others collide with. Worse, you could find that, although each component works fine, the product as a whole doesn't; you can't get from step A to step B.

Technique 147: Test with Other Applications

Category: Advice

Users rarely run just a single application. Sometimes bugs will show up when other applications are running. For example, we've run into fun bugs where a program worked fine in isolation, but when another program was running, the setup would fail. Or two programs would fight over timer messages, bringing the system to its knees.

It's easy to blame the other application when this occurs. Well, it doesn't matter whose fault it is. You have to find a way to work around it.

Technique 148: Test on All the Target Platforms

Category: Advice

If you program for Win32, test with Win98, Windows NT, and Win95. Each has its own idiosyncrasies. You may think your code will just work, but unless you actually check it out, you won't know. Likewise, check your code with as many machines, printers, and video cards as you can. You'll be surprised at the fun stuff you may find. And if it works fine, good for you. You'll sleep better.

Technique 149: Test Retail and Debug Versions

Category: Advice

It's often tempting only to test debug builds of your product; that way, if you find a bug, you can go right into the debugger and get lots of information about the problem. You are much better off testing both debug and retail builds. The retail build is what the customer will be using, and sometimes the retail and debug builds behave differently. If a bug shows up only in a retail version, not in the debug version, it's usually an uninitialized variable on the stack or a buffer overflow due to an uninitialized stack variable that is used for the buffer size.

Likewise, optimized code may show bugs that unoptimized code doesn't.

CHAPTER 16

Specific Debugging Stuff

IN THIS CHAPTER, WE WALK THROUGH some specific techniques for debugging programs, from handling first chance exceptions to tracing the stack.

Technique 150: Loading DLLs for Debugging

Category: How to

Steps

When debugging, you may need to load additional DLLs. To do so, do the following:

1. Select Project → Settings.

2. Click on the Debug tab.

3. Select Additional DLLs from the Category drop down.

4. Click on the Modules list box.

5. Either type in the name of the DLL or click on the . . . button to browse for DLLs to add.

Technique 151: Loading Executables for Debugging

Category: How to

Steps

When debugging DLLs, you need to specify the executable to load, which you do as follows:

1. Select File → Open Workspace.

2. Select Executable Files from the Files of type drop down.

3. Select the executable that loads the DLL.

4. Click on Open.

5. Follow the steps in Technique 150 to load your DLL.

If you don't have symbols for the executable you are using to debug your DLL, Visual Studio will complain. You can ignore the warning and proceed. Of course, if you do have symbols, you may find debugging easier.

Technique 152: Casting Data

Category: How to

Steps

When you debug, you often view the value of data inside the watch window or the quick watch window. You can use casting operations on the data that you view. For example, suppose you have a void pointer called foo. To see the value of foo, you could click on the watch window and type the following:

```
foo
```

To view foo as a pointer to an int, type this instead:

```
(int *) foo
```

Technique 153: Dumping Registers and What They Mean

Category: How to

Steps

From the debug toolbar, click on the icon that has ax in it. Or, from the menu, select View → Debug windows → Registers.

The registers window will show the value of the CPU registers, such as the following:

```
EAX = 00780C80 EBX = 00550000 ECX = 00000001 EDX = 00780C10
ESI = 815A5100 EDI = 00000000 EIP = 00401040 ESP = 0065FDFC
EBP = 0065FE38 EFL = 00000212 CS = 0157 DS = 015F ES = 015F
SS = 015F FS = 495F GS = 0000 OV=0 UP=0 EI=1 PL=0 ZR=0 AC=1
PE=0 CY=0 ST0 = -5.61093706791417901e-0001
ST1 = -5.61826173722854705e-0001
ST2 = +4.22371816635131835e+0000
ST3 = -3.78935062326490900e-0003
ST4 = -9.59999999999999964e+0000
ST5 = +1.37599999999999994e+0002
ST6 = +1.37599999999999994e+0002
ST7 = +0.00000000000000000e+0000 CTRL = 027F STAT = 0000
TAGS = FFFF EIP = 00000000 CS = 0000 DS = 0000
EDO = 00000000
```

Some registers tend to be more interesting than others when debugging. Usually, pointers or values in pointers are loaded into EAX. EAX is also used to store temporary results and to return values from function calls. ECX is usually used inside loops, such as by the repnz command. ECX and EDX are often used for temporary registers. Arithmetic and logical operators will invariably change the contents of EAX, ECX, and EDX. EIP, the instruction pointer, points to the current instruction being executed. ESI and EDI are used for pointer arithmetic and during loops. If you have an access violation and the EIP is on a repnz, movsw, or some other move or swap instruction, examine the ECX, ESI, and EDI registers to see where they are pointing. They will likely show you the problem. ESP is the stack register. EBP is the stack frame register. You will use ESP and EBP when you do a stack trace.

As an example, suppose that, while you are running your program, you get an access violation. Pop into the debugger and view the registers. If EAX is null, that's a good indicator that you just ran into a null pointer.

Technique 154: Switching to Hex Display

Category: How to

Steps

1.   Right click in the Watch window.

2.   Select Hexadecimal display.

Technique 155: Handling First-Chance Exceptions

Category: How to

Steps

When you encounter a first-chance exception, Visual C++ will display a message in the debug window, typically at the bottom of the screen. Note the exception code displayed there.

1. Select Debug → Exceptions. (Note that this menu option is only enabled during debugging.)

2. Scroll down the list of exceptions until you find the one you encountered.

3. Change the Action setting to Stop always.

4. Restart the debugging session by selecting Debug → Restart.

You'll now break into the debugger when the exception is encountered. You can then trace the stack, examine the data, and use your normal debugging techniques to see what caused the exception.

Technique 156: Break on Data Changed

Category: How to

Steps

This is a useful technique to employ when you know that memory is getting corrupted or that a variable has a wrong value, but you are not sure what is causing the problem. The reason could be a simple mistake, or it could be something as tricky as a buffer overrun.

1. Select Edit → Breakpoints.

2. Click on the Data tab.

3. Enter the expression to cause a breakpoint. For example, enter sz if you want to break when the value of the sz variable changes. Enter sz = 3 if you want to break when sz gets set to 3.

Caveat

Breaking when a value changes is a very powerful technique. Visual C++ does not use hardware breakpoints for this. It will significantly slow down your execution speed, and it may even take several minutes for Visual C++ to respond after you begin debugging. Thus, even though this technique can help you find very serious, hard-to-track-down bugs, you shouldn't use it as a general, catch-all technique.

Single step over your code, watching your data every time you add a new line of code to your program. That way you will find bugs before they blow up in your face (see Technique 138).

Technique 157: Skipping Execution to a Particular IP

Category: How to

Steps

Sometimes you know that the value of a variable needs to be something (say, nonzero), and in order to preserve that value, you need to skip a particular line. Perhaps you suspect that a particular line is causing a bug and thus you want to skip over it. Or maybe you want to exit an endless loop without losing state. You can do so by following these steps while in the debugger:

1. Right-click on the line that you want to execute next.

2. Select Set Next Statement.

You can also change the statement about to execute by altering the EIP register from the registers window. Do so with caution, however. You can easily screw up.

Caveat

Changing the next statement won't always do sensible things to the state of registers and the call stack. For example, you can use this technique to jump out of a call without any cleanup. Doing so will result in a messed up stack. Be careful.

Technique 158: Creating and Using a MAP File

Category: How to

A map file is a text file that contains the following information about the program being linked:

- The module name, which is the base name of the file

- The time stamp from the program file header (not from the file system)

- A list of groups in the program, with each group's start address (as section:offset), length, group name, and class

- A list of public symbols, with each address (as section:offset), symbol name, flat address, and .OBJ file where the symbol is defined

- The entry point (as section:offset)

- A list of fix-ups

The map file becomes very useful when you need to debug a retail version of a program, for example, when your program crashes on a customer's machine and all you have is the stack dump and register values. Sometimes the steps to reproduce the problem are not known, so you can't do it while loading the program in the debugger. And sometimes the problem can't be reproduced in a debug build.

Likewise, you might also get stuck without debug information if you follow our advice from Chapter 15 and test both the retail and debug versions of your program before you ship them.

Whatever the reasons for not having symbolic information, it is handy to know how to use the Dr. Watson log or stack dump. This is where the map file becomes useful. You can get a fairly good idea of where your program crashed from the EIP. Look in the map file to see which function it is in.

Next, look at the offending function. See what parameters it takes, and try to generate the assembly version of the function with the same (and this is very important) compile flags as the version you are debugging. You can get a reasonable estimate by comparing the code from the stack dump and the assembly and the map file information.

Next, speak with a Hercule Poirot accent and start tracking down the problem. You can also use the map file to see what got pulled in from the CRT and how much space variables are consuming.

Be sure to look at the registers, as well. There is a lot of useful debug information in a simple stack dump of registers. Practice reading through the map file and registers so that, when you have to use these techniques to track down a problem, you will be prepared.

To generate the map file, do the following from Visual Studio:

1. Select Project → Settings.

2. Click on the Link tab.

3. Click on Generate mapfile.

From the linker command line, use the following:

```
/map:"mapfile.map"
```

Technique 159: Walking the Call Stack

Category: How to

Steps

Walking the call stack lets you understand how your code has gotten where it is. This is an advanced technique, so we'll start with an overview of calling conventions and then jump into the technique.

To begin, let's look at the code for two functions. The first, Trace, is a normal C++ function that takes two arguments. The second, TraceEllipses, takes a variable number of arguments.

```
// thiscall convention for C++ member function
373: int Trace(int i, int i1)
374: {
00401840 push ebp
00401841 mov ebp,esp
00401843 sub esp,0Ch
00401846 mov dword ptr [ebp-0Ch],ecx
375: int j=8;
00401849 mov dword ptr [j],8
376: int k=9;
00401850 mov dword ptr [k],9
377: m_i = i+j+k+i1;
00401857 mov eax,dword ptr [i]
0040185A add eax,dword ptr [j]
0040185D add eax,dword ptr [k]
```

```
00401860 add eax,dword ptr [i1]
00401863 mov ecx,dword ptr [this]
00401866 mov dword ptr [ecx],eax
378: return i;
00401868 mov eax,dword ptr [i]
379: }
0040186B mov esp,ebp
0040186D pop ebp
0040186E ret 8
// cDecl convention for C++ member function
380: int TraceEllipses(int i, ...)
381: {
00401890 push ebp
00401891 mov ebp,esp
00401893 sub esp,8
382: int j=8;
00401896 mov dword ptr [j],8
383: int k=9;
0040189D mov dword ptr [k],9
384: m_i = i+j+k;
004018A4 mov eax,dword ptr [i]
004018A7 add eax,dword ptr [j]
004018AA add eax,dword ptr [k]
004018AD mov ecx,dword ptr [this]
004018B0 mov dword ptr [ecx],eax
385: return i;
004018B2 mov eax,dword ptr [i]
386: }
004018B5 mov esp,ebp
004018B7 pop ebp
004018B8 ret
```

Here is the calling code from the main function.

```
434: int i = 0;
0040166A mov dword ptr [i],0
435:
436: st.Trace(i, 10);
00401671 push 0Ah
00401673 mov ecx,dword ptr [i]
00401676 push ecx
00401677 lea ecx,dword ptr [st]
0040167A call StackTrace::Trace(0x00401850)
```

```
437: st.TraceEllipses(i, 10);
0040167F push 0Ah
00401681 mov edx,dword ptr [i]
00401684 push edx
00401685 lea eax,dword ptr [st]
00401688 push eax
00401689 call StackTrace::TraceEllipses(0x00401890)
0040168E add esp,0Ch
```

Now let's see what the stack will look like after a call to Trace. Note that the X86 architecture convention is that the top of the stack is the lowest address:

```
12ff54 [this] ebp-0c
12ff58 [k] ebp-8
12ff5c [j] ebp-4
12ff60 [old ebp] ebp
12ff64 [return address] ebp+4
12ff68 [i] ebp+8
12ff6c [i1] ebp+0c
```

What does all of this stuff mean? Well, we're glad you asked. Being able to read through and understand the call stack is invaluable when debugging.

EBP represents the stack frame—the point of reference for calculating local variables and function parameters. The memory above the EBP (that is, everything less than the address pointed to by EBP) until the next stack frame contains the local variables. In this case, there are two local variables, j and k. The last value is the this pointer. Everything below EBP (that is, greater than the address pointed to by EBP) represents parameters to the function, except for the first four bytes (the previous or the caller's stack frame, marked as old ebp in the sample) and the four bytes following that (the return address). Parameters are pushed in the right-to-left order in which they appear on the C++ definition of the function. In this example, you can see the i and i1 parameters to Trace. The right-most parameter is pushed on the stack first, so it appears lowest on the stack.

Note that the stack trace shown here is for the thiscall convention—the default convention for C++ member functions that do not use variable length arguments (using the . . . convention). The thiscall convention assumes that the callee cleans up the arguments. If . . . are used, however, the caller is expected to clean up the stack. When . . . are used, there is also a difference in the way the this pointer is pushed. In the thiscall convention, the this pointer is pushed as in the example just shown, after all the local variables are allocated. That is, this is pushed by the callee and is passed by the caller in ECX. Looking at the sample code, you can see that, for Trace, the function ends with a ret 8 to take care of the two parameters passed.

By contrast, with the cDecl convention, the this pointer is pushed onto the stack by the caller. Looking at the sample code, you can see that, for TraceEllipse, the function simply does a ret when it ends. Note, however, that the code that calls TraceEllipse adds 0C to the ESP to account for the two parameters the caller is passing and the this pointer. (Why 0C? Four bytes for each parameter, plus four bytes for the this pointer.)

It can sometimes be confusing to examine values on the stack frame because of the way memory is stored. For example, suppose you are at a breakpoint. You look at the EBP register to find the stack frame. Going above this stack frame gives you local variables. For example, if EBP equals 0x512ff60, the first local variable is at 0x12ff5c and spans up to 12ff60. Suppose the value stored at memory location 0x12ff5c is 0x12456098. When you dump the memory at 0x12ff5c, it will look like this:

```
0x12ff5c 98 60 45 12
```

In other words, the data is displayed using the little endian convention. The address points to the least-significant byte of the word.

To find the this pointer, look where ECX is stored at the beginning of the function.

To get to the stack frame of the caller, take the value of the address pointed to by EBP. This is a pointer to the previous stack frame. As with any stack frame, the parameters to the call are stored in the memory above the address pointed to, and the local variables are stored below what is pointed to. If you get the value stored in the address pointed to, you now have the pointer to the stack frame of the next caller. You can continue this all the way up.

Caveat

This technique is for X86 architectures. The code shown is not optimized. Optimized code will look different. For example, registers might be used instead of local variables.

Technique 160: Fixing the Call Stack If You Can't See Everything

Category: How to

Steps

Sometimes you see only part of the stack. This could be due to any one of several problems. For example, the stack could be corrupted, preventing you from tracing back. If you know which location is corrupted, you may be able to put a Data breakpoint on that location and from that, figure out what code is overwriting the stack. Usually, however, you will need to go through every line of code until you find what is causing the problem. This is one of the nastiest types of bugs to find.

Another problem could be that, beyond the stack, you run into the loader code. In this case, what you see on the stack is all that you have for debugging. Use classical debugging techniques and find out the cause of the bug you are trying to fix.

A third problem could be that you have assembly functions that do not follow a convention that the debugger can understand. (The debugger's Call Stack window is filled using the steps discussed in the previous technique.) If there is assembly code that won't let the debugger walk the EBP to find the stack trace, the debugger will throw up its hands and give up.

If you are patient, you can get past the assembly code to continue walking the stack. Before you start, write down the value in the EBP register. Next, find the value in the EBP. Go up to the point where the chain is not broken. Now start going up the stack values and find a value that looks like it is in the EBP chain. (How will you know? It should point to a similar area on the stack as the previous EBP.) Put this value in the EBP register and select View → Debug Windows → Call Stack. If the compiler shows you a meaningful stack trace to the beginning of the program (for example, to main or WinMain), then you are done. You now have enough information to continue debugging. If not, try the next value down on the stack (that is, going up memory addresses) that closely matches the EBP. Because EBP values increase as you go down the stack, ignore anything that's less than the last valid EBP stack frame. Because code is DWORD aligned, addresses must be even numbered. Thus, ignore odd numbers.

Once you have figured out what is causing the problem, you can often learn which Win32 call prevented the stack trace from working. Many times, your arguments to the function are what caused the bug. Although this technique won't always solve your problems, it can often save you days and days of debugging time.

Part II

Sample Code

WELCOME TO PART II. IN THIS SECTION, WE'LL look at complete programs that illustrate algorithms you might find useful. These programs are the source for most of the techniques discussed in Part I. We'll briefly discuss how and why we did what we did so that you can understand why a particular technique, say smart pointers, is worth understanding.

CHAPTER 17

Smart Pointers

SMART POINTERS ARE VERY USEFUL CRITTERS. A smart pointer is a templatized class that automatically takes care of memory deletion. When the class goes out of scope, the memory is deleted. No more careless memory leaks.

Smart pointers are a fairly simple concept. You create a templatized class for smart pointers so that you can use the pointers to point to any type.

You declare smart pointers the same way you would use any other pointer. Only instead of using code such as the following,

```
int *pi;
```

you use code such as this:

```
BaseSmartPointer<int> pi;
```

Unlike a normal pointer, however, the smart pointer is an object. Thus, when the local variable goes out of scope, the class's destructor is called. The smart pointer's destructor frees the memory pointed to, as shown in the following code:

```
virtual ~BaseSmartPointer()
    {
        if(m_pt)
            delete m_pt;
        m_pt = NULL;
    }
```

We have created two smart pointer classes. The first, BaseSmartPointer, is for intrinsic types such as int, float, and so forth. It does not supply a -> operator. The second, ObjectSmartPointer, derives from BaseSmartPointer and provides a -> operator.

Files

Here are the actual source code listings for the smart pointer files. Smartptr.h is the header file and Smartptr.cpp is the code file. The technique numbers in the comments refer to techniques in Part I. You can find these files and a corresponding

Visual C++ project file in the smartptr folder on this book's accompanying CD-ROM.

Smartptr.h

```cpp
#include <stdio.h>
//Technique 58
//Technique 60


template <class T> class BaseSmartPointer
{
private:
   // Copy ctor and = operator are private to prevent pointer from being copied
   // from one smart pointer to another.
   BaseSmartPointer<T>&operator=(BaseSmartPointer<T>&bsp)
   {
      return *this;
   }

   BaseSmartPointer(BaseSmartPointer<T>&bsp)
   {
   }
protected:
   T   *m_pt;
public:
   BaseSmartPointer(T *pt=NULL) : m_pt(pt)
   {
   }

   virtual ~BaseSmartPointer()
   {
      if(m_pt)
         delete m_pt;
      m_pt = NULL;
   }

   T &operator*() const
   {
      return *m_pt;
   }

   T*operator=(T *pt)
   {
      if(m_pt)
         delete m_pt;
```

```
        m_pt = pt;
        return m_pt;
    }

};

//TIP 59
template <class T> class ObjectSmartPointer : public BaseSmartPointer <T>
{
private:
    // Make this private so someone can't use the copy ctor
    ObjectSmartPointer(ObjectSmartPointer<T>&osp)
    {
    }

public:
    ObjectSmartPointer(T* pt=NULL) : BaseSmartPointer<T>(pt)
    {
    }

    T* operator=(T *pt)
    {
        return BaseSmartPointer<T>::operator=(pt);
    }

    T *operator->() const
    {
        return m_pt;
    }
};
class foo
{
public:
    int i;
    float f;
};
```

Smartptr.cpp

```
#include "smartptr.h"
#include "iostream.h"
void TestSmartPointer(void)
```

```
{
    BaseSmartPointer<int> pi;
    ObjectSmartPointer<foo> po;

    po = new foo;
    po->i = 10;
    po->f = 10.5;
    cout << (*po).i << " " << po->f << "\n";
    pi = new int;
    pi = new int;
    *pi = 100;
    cout << *pi << "\n";


#ifdef COMPILE_ERROR
    //Technique 93
    // Neither of these will compile because we made the ctor and = operator
    // private.
    ObjectSmartPointer<foo> po2(po);
    ObjectSmartPointer<foo> po1;

    po1 = po;
    cout << po1->i;
#endif

}

int main(int argc, char *argv[])
{
    TestSmartPointer();
    return 0;
}
```

CHAPTER 18

Reference Counting

REFERENCE COUNTING LETS YOU SAFELY SHARE OBJECTS. The concept is simple. Rather than controlling an object's lifetime externally, the object itself controls when it is deleted. Or rather, the object's lifetime is controlled indirectly from the outside via a usage count. The users of the object indicate when they start and stop using the object. The object guarantees that it will stick around as long as it is being used by someone. This is the technique used by COM objects.

Implementing this technique is simple. Before an object is used, the Add method is called on it. This increments an internal counter:

```
int Add()
{
   return ++m_cRef;
}
```

When the object is finished being used, the Release method is called. This method decrements the internal counter, and deletes the object if the counter has gone to zero:

```
int Release()
{
   int cRef;

   // Technique 86
   --m_cRef;
   cRef = m_cRef;
   if(!cRef)
      delete this;
   return cRef;
}
```

The object can be shared among many different parts of code. Each part follows the rules of calling Add and Release; thus, as long as someone is using the object, it won't be destroyed accidentally.

Note that the constructor and destructor for this class are private. That prevents the reference counted object from being created on the stack or deleted by external users of the object.

Combining reference counting and smart pointers is also a very powerful technique.

Files

Here is the actual source code listing for the reference counting example. All of the code is contained in access.cpp. The technique numbers in the comments refer to techniques in Part I. You can find these files and a corresponding Visual C++ project file in the access folder on this book's accompanying CD-ROM.

access.cpp

```cpp
#include <iostream.h>
#include <malloc.h>
#include <memory.h>



// Technique 110

class RefCounted
{
private:
    int m_cRef;
    // Made private so automatic variables can't be created.
    ~RefCounted()
    {
    }

    // Technique 93
    RefCounted() : m_cRef(1)
    {
    }

    // Technique 47
    void *operator new(size_t cbAlloc)
    {
        return malloc(cbAlloc);
    }
```

```
        void operator delete(void * pv)
        {
            free(pv);
        }
public:
    // Technique 75
    static RefCounted *newRefCounted()
    {
        return new RefCounted;
    }

    int Add()
    {
        return ++m_cRef;
    }

    int Release()
    {
        int cRef;

        // Technique 86
        --m_cRef;
        cRef = m_cRef;
        if(!cRef)
            delete this;
        return cRef;
    }

    void Hello()
    {
        cout << "RefCount = ";
        cout << m_cRef;
        cout << "\n";
    }
};

void TestRefCounted()
{
#ifdef NOCOMPILE
    RefCounted ref;
#endif
    RefCounted *pref;
```

```
        // Technique 46

    pref = RefCounted::newRefCounted();


    pref->Add();
    pref->Hello();
    pref->Release();
    pref->Hello();
    pref->Release();

}


int main(int argc, char *argv[])
{
    TestRefCounted();
    return 0;
}
```

CHAPTER 19

Dynamic Arrays

ARRAYS ARE A VERY USEFUL AND COMMON DATA STRUCTURE. They are simple, and they provide very fast look-up times. Arrays do have some limitations, however. In particular, they are fixed in size. So you always need to make sure that you stay within their bounds.

A dynamic array is like a regular array, except that it dynamically resizes. If you insert an element beyond its bounds, the array will dynamically grow. Thus, you don't need to worry about checking for index overflow or reallocating the array yourself. The dynamic array class does that for you.

We've built the dynamic array class out of two classes. The first, Drgbase, is the worker class. It contains all of the functions for indexing, copying, and expanding the arrays. It operates on void pointers so that it can work generically on any type. Of course, void pointers don't provide type safety, so there is another class, Drg, which is a templatized class privately derived from Drgbase. It provides the type safe interfaces to the dynamic array capabilities.

It is important to note that we do all of the work in Drgbase. Thus, there is very little code overhead from providing the templatized interfaces because the templatized classes will all use the common code from the nontemplatized base class (see Technique 107).

To make the class more natural to use, we overload a lot of operators for the class. For example, the following excerpt from the exp.cpp folder on this book's accompanying CD-ROM walks through a dynamic array of characters:

```
void BuildStack(Stack<char> &st, Drg <char>&drg)
{
   char ch;
   drg = 0;
   while(ch = *drg++)
   {
      st.Push(ch);
   }
}
```

The following excerpt, also from exp.cpp, sets values inside of a dynamic array:

```
Drg <char>drg;
char *pch;
int i = 0;
```

```
pch = sz;
while(drg[i] = *pch++) i++;
```

Because the base class operates on void pointers, it needs to know the size of the elements stored in the array. This is handled by the constructor for Drg, which passes in the size of the templatized type:

```
Drg() : Drgbase(sizeof(T)), m_it(0)
{
}
```

The base class uses this size to calculate all of its array look ups and memory management. For example, the following method finds the value at a particular index. Note that it computes the offset by multiplying the index by the size of each element:

```
void * Drgbase::PvAt(long lindex) const
{
    void *  pv;

    if(!m_rgb)
        return NULL;

    pv = (void *)(m_rgb + (lindex * m_lcbSize));
    if(pv < (void *)m_pbMac)
        return  pv;
    return  NULL;
}
```

As you can see in PvAppend and PvInsert, if an insert requires that the array grows, the FGrow method is called. This allocates or reallocates memory to accommodate the new size.

As you look through the code, you will see in action many of the techniques discussed in Part I. For example, we create copy constructors and overload the = operator. Within these methods, we copy the memory as well as the memory pointers. We also do a lot of checking to make sure that memory allocations were successful, and we do a lot of work with operator overloading.

Files

Here is the actual source code listing for the dynamic array example. The header file is drg.h; drg.cpp is the C++ file. The technique numbers in the comments refer to techniques in Part I. These files and a corresponding Visual C++ project file are in the exp folder on this book's accompanying CD-ROM.

drg.h

```
#ifndef _DRG_H
#define _DRG_H
#include "..\inc\tips.h"


// Technique 39
// Technique 40
#ifdef NULL
#pragma message("NULL already defined")
#else
#define NULL 0
#endif
// Some more work is needed for drgBase to be freely used. For example I don't
// check to make sure that m_rgb is not null all the time
// Also the parameter passed in to PvInsert and PvAppend is not checked. These are
// the cleanups that are expected to be done to make this part of a class library.
// I also do not put lot of asserts deliberately so as not distract from the code
// that demonstrates the techniques. But in practice it's better to assert than to
// comment.
// Technique 107
class Drgbase
{
private:
    long    m_lcbSize:16;
    long    m_lcbChunk:16;

    BYTE *  m_rgb;


    BYTE *  m_pbMac;
    BYTE *  m_pbMax;
    long    LcbMac(void)
    {
        return m_pbMac - m_rgb;
    }
    long    LIndexMac(void);
    BOOL    FGrow(void);
    void    Copy(const Drgbase &drgbase);
```

```
    public:
        Drgbase(const Drgbase &drgbase);
        const Drgbase &operator=(const Drgbase &drgbase);
        // Technique 92
        Drgbase(long lcbSize=4, long lcChunk=12);
        ~Drgbase(void);
        void * PvInsert(void * pv, long lindex);
        void * PvAppend(void * pv, long lcItem=1);
        void * PvAt(long lindex) const;
        BOOL FRemove(long lindex, void * pv);
        long LCount(void) const;
        void * PvStart(void) const;
        void * PvMac(void) const;
    };

    // Technique 107
    template <class T>
    class Drg : private Drgbase
    {
    private:
        int m_it;
    public:
        Drg() : Drgbase(sizeof(T)), m_it(0)
        {
        }

        Drg(const Drg<T> &drg) : Drgbase(drg)
        {
            m_it = drg.m_it;
        }

        // Used for iteration
        T *PStart(void)
        {
            return (T *)PvStart();
        }

        T *PMac(void)
        {
            return (T *)PvMac();
        }
```

```
long LcMac(void) const
{
    return Drgbase::LCount();
}


T &operator*(void) const
{
    return *(T *)PvAt(m_it);
}


T&operator=(int i)
{
    m_it = i;
    return operator*();
}


// Technique 101
T*operator++(void)  //Prefix
{
    return (T *)PvAt(++m_it);
}


T*operator++(int)  //Postfix
{
    return (T *)PvAt(m_it++);
}


T*operator--(void)  //Prefix
{
    return (T *)PvAt(--m_it);
}


T*operator--(int)   //Postfix
{
    return (T *)PvAt(m_it--);
}


T *Insert(const T &t, int i)
{
    return (T *)PvInsert((void *)&t, i);
}
```

```
    T *Append(const T &t)
    {
        return (T *)PvAppend((void *)&t);
    }


    BOOL FRemove(int i, T *pt)
    {
        return Drgbase::FRemove(i, pt);
    }


    BOOL FExpand(long lCount)
    {
        return (NULL == PvAppend(NULL, lCount));
    }


    T &operator[](int i)
    {
        return *(T *)PvAt(i);
    }


    const T &operator[](int i) const
    {
        return *(T *)PvAt(i);
    }
};
typedef class Drg *PDrg;

#endif //_DRG_H
```

drg.cpp

```
#include <iostream.h>
#include "drg.h"
#include <malloc.h>
#include <memory.h>
#include <string.h>

long Drgbase::LIndexMac(void)
{
    return  LcbMac() / m_lcbSize;
}
```

```
BOOL Drgbase::FGrow(void)
{
   long    lcbMac;
   long    lcbMax;
   long    lcbOffset = m_pbMax - m_rgb;
   if(NULL == m_rgb)
   {
      lcbMac = 0;
      lcbMax = m_lcbChunk;
      m_rgb = (BYTE *)malloc(lcbMax);
   }
   else
   {
      lcbMac = LcbMac();
      lcbMax = (m_pbMax - m_rgb) + m_lcbChunk;
      m_rgb = (BYTE *)realloc(m_rgb, lcbMax);
   }
   if(m_rgb)
   {
      // Technique 54
      memset(m_rgb+lcbOffset,  0, m_lcbChunk);
      m_pbMac = m_rgb + lcbMac;
      m_pbMax = m_rgb + lcbMax;
      return TRUE;
   }
   return  FALSE;
}

void    Drgbase::Copy(const Drgbase &drgbase)
{
   long lcb;

   // Technique 55
   if(&drgbase == this)
      return;

   m_lcbSize = drgbase.m_lcbSize;
   m_lcbChunk = drgbase.m_lcbChunk;
   m_rgb = (BYTE *)malloc(lcb = (drgbase.m_pbMac- drgbase.m_rgb));
   if(m_rgb)
   {
      memcpy(m_rgb, drgbase.m_rgb, lcb);
      m_pbMac = m_pbMax = m_rgb+lcb;
   }
}
```

```
Drgbase::Drgbase(const Drgbase &drgbase)
{
    Copy(drgbase);
}


const Drgbase &Drgbase::operator=(const Drgbase &drgbase)
{
    // In real world you might want to check the buffer size and reuse if you can
    // before reallocating.
    if(m_rgb)
        free(m_rgb);
    Copy(drgbase);
    return *this;
}



Drgbase::Drgbase(long lcbSize, long lcChunk)
{
    m_lcbSize = lcbSize;
    m_lcbChunk = lcChunk * lcbSize;
    m_pbMac = m_pbMax = m_rgb = NULL;
}


Drgbase::~Drgbase(void)
{
    if(m_rgb)
        free(m_rgb);
    m_rgb = m_pbMac = m_pbMax = NULL;
}


void * Drgbase::PvAppend(void * pv, long lcItem)
{
    long lcbItem;
    void *pvRet;


    if((lcbItem = lcItem * m_lcbSize) > m_lcbChunk)
    {
        // If the number of items being appended is > the chunk size, grow the
        // chunk size before making space in m_rgb
        m_lcbChunk = lcbItem;
    }
    if(m_pbMac+lcbItem >= m_pbMax && !FGrow())
        goto LFail;
```

```
      pvRet = m_pbMac;
      if(pv)
      {
          while(lcItem)
          {
             memcpy(m_pbMac, pv, m_lcbSize);
             --lcItem;
             m_pbMac+=m_lcbSize;
          }
      }
      else
      {
          // If no data is passed initialize with 0s.
          memset(m_pbMac, 0, lcbItem);
          m_pbMac += lcbItem;
      }
      return pvRet;
LFail:
      return  NULL;
}


void * Drgbase::PvInsert(void * pv, long lindex)
{
      BYTE *  pbLindex;

      pbLindex = m_rgb + (lindex * m_lcbSize);

      if(pbLindex < m_pbMac)
      {
          // Index within the range.
          // See if there is a need to grow the array
          if(m_pbMac == m_pbMax && !FGrow())
             goto LFail;
          // We have enough room to do the insert
          // Shift the array by m_lcbSize
          // memmove makes sure overlapping areas can be copied. So no need to worry
          // about that.
          memmove((BYTE *)(pbLindex + m_lcbSize), pbLindex, m_pbMac - pbLindex);
          memcpy(pbLindex, pv, m_lcbSize);
          pv = pbLindex;
          m_pbMac += m_lcbSize;
      }
```

```
        else
        {
            // Can't obviously insert beyond the last one. Append instead
            return PvAppend(pv);
        }
        return pv;
LFail:
    return  NULL;
}


void * Drgbase::PvAt(long lindex) const
{
    void *  pv;

    if(!m_rgb)
        return NULL;

    pv = (void *)(m_rgb + (lindex * m_lcbSize));
    if(pv < (void *)m_pbMac)
        return  pv;
    return  NULL;
}


long Drgbase::LCount(void) const
{
    return  ((m_pbMac - m_rgb)/m_lcbSize);
}


BOOL Drgbase::FRemove(long lindex, void * pv)
{
    void * pvT;
    long lcbToBlt;

    pvT = PvAt(lindex);
    if(!pvT)
        return FALSE;
    if(pv)
    {
        // If input buffer is given then
        // Copy the data into the input buffer
        memcpy(pv, pvT, m_lcbSize);
    }
```

```
    m_pbMac -= m_lcbSize;
    lcbToBlt = m_pbMac - (BYTE *)pvT;
    if(lcbToBlt)
    {
        // If it isn't the last one being removed shift the array back
        memcpy(pvT, (BYTE *)pvT+m_lcbSize, lcbToBlt);
    }
    return TRUE;
}

void * Drgbase::PvStart(void) const
{
    return m_rgb;
}

void * Drgbase::PvMac(void) const
{
    return m_pbMac;
}
```

CHAPTER 20

Strings

ONE WAY OR ANOTHER, ALMOST ALL APPLICATIONS PROCESS STRINGS. Visual C++ comes with an implementation of the ANSI string class. This is an extremely rich string class that does everything you could want and then some. In this chapter, we've provided implementation of a lighter weight, smaller, and less functional string class. It provides the basic capabilities you need: copying, comparing, and appending. It doesn't do all the fancy stuff, and it doesn't support Unicode.

Although this code does not illustrate complex algorithms, it does provide examples for many of the techniques discussed in Part I; it also demonstrates a lot of operator overloading.

For example, the following code overloads += so that += can be used to perform string appending. Note that two versions are supplied. One takes a String class. The other takes a char *. When you write your own operator overloading, be sure likewise to overload for all of the various types your operators might logically take as operands:

```
const String& operator+=(const String& string)
    {
       Append(string.m_pch, string.m_cch);
       return *this;
    }

    const String& operator+=(const char *sz)
    {
       Append(sz, strlen(sz));
       return *this;
    }
```

Files

Here is the actual source code listing for the string class example. The C++ file is String.cpp. The technique numbers in the comments refer to techniques in Part I. These files and a corresponding Visual C++ project file are in the String folder on this book's accompanying CD-ROM.

String.cpp

```cpp
#include <stdio.h>
#include <memory.h>
#include <string.h>
#include <iostream.h>

/*
Caveats in this class are we do not deal with UNICODE text or any type of extended
ASCII text. For example, this class cannot handle double byte strings as you would
encounter in the Far East languages or Arabic alphabet which is bidirectional.
We also do not provide extensive error checking for parameters. If you pass null
for the sz in the constructor below the code GPFs. Doing any operator like = or >
on an empty string will result in predictable but disastrous results like GPF. We
could instead make it return something but it's better to GPF than fail in benign
way and not let the caller know about it. It will hide a potential bug in the
caller's code which might have other side effects that won't be as obvious as the
GPF this produces. If you want to use this code for a class library where you may
not have control over the caller's actions, you need to make it fail benignly and
have an error mechanism or have it throw exceptions. You can also assert. But it's
always better to deal with the exception than to simply assert.
*/


class String
{
private:
    // Added const member only to demonstrate initialization of const members.
    const int m_cchTest;
    // length of the string
    int m_cch;
    // null terminated string. Makes it easy to give out null terminated strings.
    char *m_pch;

    // Technique 56
    void InitString(const char *pch, int cch);
    void Append(const char *pch, int cch);
    void ReinitString(const char *pch, int cch);
public:
    // Technique 69
    // Technique 70
```

```
// Technique 91
String(void) : m_cch(0), m_cchTest(10)
{
    m_pch =NULL;
    // Technique 71
    // m_cchTest = 10; Not OK
}


// Technique 94
String(const String &string): m_cchTest(10)
{
    InitString(string.m_pch, string.m_cch);
}


String(char *sz): m_cchTest(10)
{
    InitString(sz, strlen(sz));
}


~String(void)
{
    // Technique 50
    if(m_pch)
        delete m_pch;
}


char & operator[](int i)
{
    // if i < 0 or >= cch then it will cause access violation just like
    // normal arrays.
    return m_pch[i];
}


const char& operator[](int i) const
{
    // if i < 0 or >= cch then it will cause access violation just like
    // normal arrays.
    return m_pch[i];
}


// Technique 77
const String& operator=(const String &string)
{
```

```
    // Technique 78
    if(&string != this)
        ReinitString(string.m_pch, string.m_cch);
    return *this;
}

const String& operator=(const char *sz)
{
    ReinitString(sz, strlen(sz));
    return *this;
}

const String& operator+=(const String& string)
{
    Append(string.m_pch, string.m_cch);
    return *this;
}

const String& operator+=(const char *sz)
{
    Append(sz, strlen(sz));
    return *this;
}

int operator==(const String& string) const
{
    return(strcmp(m_pch, string.m_pch) == 0);
}

int operator==(const char *sz) const
{
    return(strcmp(m_pch, sz) == 0);
}

int operator>(const String& string) const
{
    return(strcmp(m_pch, string.m_pch) > 0);
}

int operator>(const char *sz) const
{
    return(strcmp(m_pch, sz) > 0);
}
```

```
    int operator<(const String& string) const
    {
        return(strcmp(m_pch, string.m_pch) < 0);
    }


    int operator<(const char *sz) const
    {
        return(strcmp(m_pch, sz) < 0);
    }


    // Technique 53
#ifdef CODE_GPF
    String &operator+(const String&string) const
    {
        String stringNew(m_pch);

        stringNew.Append(string.m_pch, string.m_cch);
        return stringNew;
    }
#endif

    String operator+(const String&string) const
    {
        String stringNew(m_pch);

        stringNew.Append(string.m_pch, string.m_cch);
        return stringNew;
    }
};


// Technique 56
void String::InitString(const char * pch, int cch)
{
    m_cch = 0;
    m_pch = NULL;
    if(cch)
    {
        m_pch = new char[cch+1];
        if(m_pch)
        {
            strcpy(m_pch, pch);
            m_cch = cch;
        }
    }
}
```

```
void String::Append(const char *pch, int cch)
{
    char *pchNew;
    int cchNew;


    // Technique 18
    // Technique 79
    if(!cch)
        return;
    if(!m_pch)
    {
        // If this is empty string, then just initialize it with this string.
        InitString(pch, cch);
        return;
    }
    // Allocate an extra character for the null terminator at the end
    cchNew = m_cch + cch;
    pchNew = new char[cchNew + 1];

    // Technique 49
    if(!pchNew)
        return;
    // Successfully allocated new buffer
    strcpy(pchNew, m_pch);

    // Technique 128
    strcpy(pchNew+m_cch, pch);
    if(m_pch)
        delete m_pch;
    m_pch = pchNew;
    m_cch = cchNew;
}

void String::ReinitString(const char *pch, int cch)
{
    char *pchOld;
    int cchOld;


    if(cch != m_cch)
    {
        pchOld = m_pch;
        cchOld = m_cch;
```

```
        InitString(pch, cch);
        if(m_pch)
        {
            // Successfully Inited the string? Now we can delete the memory for
            // the old pch if there was one.
            if(pchOld)
                delete pchOld;
        }
        else
        {
            // Failed to allocate space for the string? Restore the old values.
            m_pch = pchOld;
            m_cch = cchOld;
        }
    }
    else
    {
        // If the length of the string is the same, then no need to reallocate the
        // buffer.
        strcpy(m_pch, pch);
    }
}

void PrintConstString(const String &string)
{
    int i = 0;
    while(string[i])
    {
        cout << string[i];
        // Technique 80
        // NOCOMPILE the following won't compile if you remove the comments.
        // string[i] = ' ';
        i++;
    }
    cout << '\n';
}

void PrintString(String &string)
{
    int i = 0;
    while(string[i])
    {
        cout << string[i];
        // Unlike above this compiles.
```

```
            string[i] = ' ';
            i++;
        }
    }

void TestStringClass(void)
{
    String string("Test");
    String string1(string);
    String string2;


    string1 = "Test1";
    string1 += string;
    string ="zing";
    // Technique 105
    PrintConstString(string);

    if(string1 == string)
        string1 = "equal";
    else if(string1 < string)
        string1 = "less";
    else
        string1 = "greater";
    PrintConstString(string);
    PrintConstString(string1);
    string2 = string + string1;
    PrintConstString(string2);
}

int main(int argc, char *argv[])
{
    TestStringClass();


    return 0;
}
```

Bit Manipulation

THERE ARE MANY CASES WHEN ONE WANTS TO MANIPULATE BIT FIELDS. Bit fields are useful for compact representation of information, thus reducing memory footprint. They are often used with hardware devices and computer graphics, and they are also useful with many fundamental algorithms.

The bits class shown in this file provides many methods for manipulating bit fields. The class is written to operate on bit fields of any length. The member variable m_cbit indicates how many bits are in the bit field. The actual bits are stored in a series of DWORDs in the m_rgdw array.

It is important to remember when looking at this code that, because the class operates on bit fields of any length, the methods break bit manipulation into DWORD-size chunks. For example, the Get method determines if a particular bit is set. The routine finds which DWORD the requested bit is in by dividing the bit number by the number of bits in a DWORD, as follows:

```
idw = ibit / cbitDWORD;
```

It then creates a mask field for the bit and uses bitwise AND to determine if that bit is set, as shown here:

```
if(m_rgdw[idw] & DwMask(ibit))
    return(TRUE);
```

DwMask returns a bit mask for a specific bit. As with the calculation shown in Get, this operates on bit fields of any length. So we first determine the bit location within the DWORD. Here, we use the mod function to find the offset within the desired bit field. We then use a shift to construct the mask:

```
return 01L << (ibit % cbitDWORD);
```

The rest of the code is straightforward and uses nice, efficient techniques for moving bits around in fields (for example, see ShiftLeft) and for getting and setting bits. You can look through this code during your copious spare time.

Files

Here is the actual source code listing for the bits class example. The C++ file is
bits.cpp. The technique numbers in the comments refer to techniques in Part I.
These files and a corresponding Visual C++ project file are in the bits folder on
the accompanying disk. You can find a version of bits that uses the drg class on
the Essential Techniques Web site, www.essentialtechniques.com.

bits.cpp

```cpp
#include <stdio.h>
#include <memory.h>
#include <string.h>
#include <iostream.h>
#include "..\inc\tips.h"


// Technique 28
const int cbitDWORD  = sizeof(DWORD) * 8;


// Rotate cBits bits in the given DWORD. The return value from the function is the
// resulting DWORD after rotate.
DWORD RotateLeft(DWORD dw, int cBits)
{
    // Code generated
    /*
    0040E813    mov         eax,dword ptr [dw]
    0040E816    mov         ecx,dword ptr [cBits]
    0040E819    shl         eax,cl
    sizeof(DWORD) * 8 is 32 bytes  which is 20h.
    0040E81B    mov         ecx,20h
    0040E820    sub         ecx,dword ptr [cBits]
    0040E823    mov         edx,dword ptr [dw]
    0040E826    shr         edx,cl
    0040E828    or          eax,edx

    */

    // Shift the DWORD left by cBits and then OR it with the result of shifting
    // the DWORD right by the size of DWORD in bits minus cBits.
    return (dw << cBits) | (dw >> (sizeof(DWORD)*8 - cBits));
}
```

```
DWORD RotateRight(DWORD dw, int cBits)
{
    return (dw >> cBits) | (dw << (sizeof(DWORD)*8 - cBits));
}


// Class that lets you manipulate variable length bit field
// Technique 32
class BF
{
public:
    BF();
    ~BF();
private:

    DWORD *m_rgdw; // Array of allocated DWORDs for the bits
    DWORD m_cbit;  // Number of bits for this bitfield class. Set using FSetSize
                   // function
    DWORD m_cdw;   // Number of DWORDs. The number of bits is rounded to the
                   // nearest DWORD. At most 3 bits are wasted.

    DWORD DwMask(DWORD ibit); // Method to get the mask used to get the bit after
                              // the appropriate DWORD in the array is located
    void ShiftLeftBits(DWORD cBits, DWORD cDwords);
public:
    BOOL  FSetSize(DWORD cBitNeeded);   // This must be called at least once before
                                        // the class can be used.
    BOOL  Get(DWORD ibit);              // Returns TRUE if the i'th bit is set.
                                        // Returns FALSE otherwise
    void  Set(DWORD ibit, BOOL fVal);   // Sets the i'th bit to the value in fVal.
    void  PrintBits(void);
    void  ShiftLeft(DWORD cbitShift);     // Shift left by ibit number bits. Fill
                                          // the least significant ibit bits with 0s
};

BF::BF() : m_cbit(0), m_rgdw(NULL), m_cdw(0)
{
}
```

```
BF::~BF()
{
    // Technique 64
    if(m_rgdw)
        delete [] m_rgdw;
}


BOOL  BF::FSetSize(DWORD cbitNeeded)
{
    DWORD *pdw;
    long cdw;

    // Always allocate to the nearest 4 bytes by rounding
    cdw = (cbitNeeded + cbitDWORD - 1)/ cbitDWORD;
    // Technique 19
    // Technique 49
    // Technique 51
    pdw = new DWORD[cdw];
    if(pdw)
    {
        // Technique 50
        // Technique 52
        if(m_rgdw)
            delete [] m_rgdw;
        // Technique 54
        memset(pdw, 0L, sizeof(DWORD) * cdw);

        m_rgdw = pdw;
        m_cdw = cdw;
        m_cbit = cbitNeeded;
        return TRUE;
    }
    return FALSE;
}


DWORD BF::DwMask(DWORD  ibit)
{
    return 01L << (ibit % cbitDWORD);
}


BOOL  BF::Get(DWORD  ibit)
{
    DWORD    idw;
```

```
    // Technique 18
    // Returns FALSE if you ask for a bit that does not exist or FSetSize has
    // never been called
    if(ibit >= m_cbit || 0 == m_cbit)
        return(FALSE);


    // Technique 124

    /* Code generated for the following
    0040F127    mov         eax,dword ptr [ibit]
    0040F12A    shr         eax,5
    0040F12D    mov         dword ptr [idw],eax
    */

    idw = ibit / cbitDWORD;

    if(m_rgdw[idw] & DwMask(ibit))
        return(TRUE);
    return(FALSE);
}

void  BF::Set(DWORD  ibit, BOOL  fVal)
{
    int    idw;
    DWORD dwMask;

    if(ibit >= m_cbit || 0 == m_cbit)
        return;
    idw = ibit / cbitDWORD;
    dwMask = DwMask(ibit);
    if(fVal)
        m_rgdw[idw] |= dwMask;
    else
        m_rgdw[idw] &= (~dwMask);
}

// Shift m_rgl by cBits for cdws DWORDs.
void BF::ShiftLeftBits(DWORD cBits, DWORD cdws)
{
    DWORD *pdw;
    DWORD *pdwMac;
    DWORD dwCarry;
    DWORD cBitsRight = cbitDWORD - cBits;
```

```
        pdw = m_rgdw;
        pdwMac = pdw + cdws;

        while(pdw < pdwMac)
        {
            // Calculate the dwCarry that comes from the next DWORD into this DWORD
            // when shifted
            dwCarry =
                (pdw+1 == pdwMac) ?
                dwCarry = 0 :                        // No bits to get since this //
                                                     // is the last long
                dwCarry = *(pdw + 1)<<cBitsRight;    // Shift the cBits from the //
                                                     // next long into the least //
                                                     // significant position

            // Now shift the long right. Why shift right? Because on X86 the bits are
            // going left to right.
            // The array of m_rgl is all bits that flow from left to right, like
            // little endian byte ordering.
            // Move the bits from lCarry into the space left by this shift.
            *pdw >>= cBits;
            *pdw |= dwCarry;
            // Technique 22
            ++pdw;
        }
    }


void  BF::ShiftLeft(DWORD cbitShift)
{
    DWORD lcdw;
    DWORD lcBits;
    DWORD lcdwUnchanged = m_cdw;

    // Generate error or have a bool return value so failure can be indicated to
    // the caller in real application scenarios.
    if(0 == m_cbit)
        return;

    if(cbitShift < 0)
        return;
    // This saves the code below from having to deal with lcdwUnchanged becoming
    // negative etc.
    // It also saves us from doing extra shifting.
    if(cbitShift > m_cbit)
        cbitShift = m_cbit;
```

```
      // Calculate the number of bytes to shift
      if(lcdw = (cbitShift / cbitDWORD))
      {

          // Number of DWORDs that are unchanged but must be moved left
          lcdwUnchanged = m_cdw - lcdw;
          // memmove moves bytes so multiply lcdwUnchanged by the size of DWORD to
          // get the bytes to move left
          memmove(m_rgdw, m_rgdw + lcdw, lcdwUnchanged * sizeof(DWORD));
          memset(m_rgdw + lcdwUnchanged, 0L, lcdw*sizeof(DWORD));
      }
      // Get how many bits left to move
      if(lcBits = cbitShift % cbitDWORD)
      {
          // For the bits that are not whole DWORDs, call the method that moves them
          // a partial amount across lcb+1 DWORDs.
          // The +1 is there since there has to be at least one long that needs to
          // be adjusted. Notice that lcb is the result of truncation
          ShiftLeftBits(lcBits, lcdwUnchanged);
      }
}


void BF::PrintBits(void)
{
    DWORD i;
    cout << "*******\n";
    for(i=0;i<m_cbit;i++)
    {
        cout << Get(i);

        // Technique 34
        if(!((i+1) % 64))
            cout <<"\n";
    }
}


// Test program that uses the bitfield. Sets the size to be 256 bits
// Sets every 3rd bit in the bitfield to 1
// Then for every bit in the bitfield it prints 1 if it's on and 0 if it's off. It
// prints 16 bits per line.
void TestBF()
```

```
    {
        BF bf;
        DWORD i;
        DWORD cSize = 256;

        bf.FSetSize(cSize);
        bf.Set(cSize-1, TRUE);
        bf.PrintBits();
        for(i=0;i<cSize;i++)
        {
            bf.ShiftLeft(1);
        }
        bf.PrintBits();
        for(i=0;i<cSize;i++)
            if(i % 3)
                bf.Set(i, TRUE);
        bf.PrintBits();
        bf.FSetSize(cSize);
        bf.Set(cSize-1, TRUE);
        bf.ShiftLeft(cSize/2);
        bf.PrintBits();
        if(bf.Get(cSize/2-1))
            cout << "bit set\n";
        else
            cout << "bit not set\n";
    }

int main(int argc, char *argv[])
{
    TestBF();
    cout << hex << RotateLeft(0x5555aaaa, 20) << ' ';//aaa555a
    cout << RotateRight(0x5555aaaa, 20) << '\n';//5aaaa555
    return 0;
}
```

CHAPTER 22

Sorting

THERE ARE A MILLION DIFFERENT WAYS TO SORT. Okay, we exaggerate. There are a few hundred. But as a programmer, you are expected to memorize them all. Each sorting algorithm has its own performance characteristics. In this sample, we've implemented a classic algorithm called "quicksort," as well as a binary-search algorithm. We aren't suggesting that either of these techniques will be the ultimate solution for your problems. But they can be a useful starting point.

Files

Here is the actual source code listing for the sorting file. The code file is bsrch.cpp. The technique numbers in the comments refer to techniques in Part I. You can find the file and a corresponding Visual C++ project file in the algorithms folder on this book's accompanying CD-ROM.

bsrch.cpp

```cpp
#include <assert.h>
#include <iostream.h>
#include <memory.h>
#include <string.h>
#include "algor.h"

void SArray::Dump(void)
{
    for(int i=0; i<m_clMac; i++)
    {
        cout << m_rgl[i];
        cout << " ";
    }
    cout << "\n";
}

// If it is already there in the array return its index
// If it is not there, insert it and return its index
```

```
// If the array is full then it returns -1
int SArray::IndexInsert(long l)
{
    int il;

    il = IndexFind(l);
    if(il != m_clMac)
    {
        if(m_rgl[il] == l)
            return il;
        if(clMax == m_clMac)
            return -1;
        // It is not found and there is space to insert it.
        memmove(m_rgl+il+1, m_rgl+il, (m_clMac - il)*sizeof(long));
    }
    m_rgl[il] = l;
    ++m_clMac;
    return il;
}


// Binary search and return index for a position where the value is either equal
// to or less than the key being searched.
int SArray::IndexFind(long l)
{
    // Technique 17
    int iLeft = 0;
    int iRight = m_clMac;
    int iMiddle;
    long lM;

    if(m_clMac == 0)
        return 0;

    while(iLeft < iRight)
    {
        iMiddle = (iLeft + iRight)/2;
        lM = m_rgl[iMiddle];
        if(l < lM)
            iRight = iMiddle;
        else if(l > lM)
            iLeft = iMiddle+1;
        else
            return iMiddle;
    }
```

```
    // This means iLeft >= iRight
    return iLeft;
}

void SArray::UnsortedInsert(long l)
{
    m_rgl[m_clMac] = l;
    ++m_clMac;
}

void SArray::QuickSort(int iLeft, int iRight)
{
    long lKey;
    int i;
    int j;
    long lT=0;

    if(iLeft < iRight)
    {
        i = iLeft-1;
        lKey = m_rgl[iRight];
        j = iRight;

        while(i < j)
        {
            // Note the pre-increment and pre-decrement below.
            // This means the increment/decrement is done before the value is
            // checked.

            while(m_rgl[++i] < lKey);
            // Technique 30
            // There is no way i can go past the right bound because lKey is
            // picked to be the right most entry.
            // So we simply assert which does not cost anything in the retail
            // version.
            assert(i < m_clMac);

            do
            {
                // Technique 65
                j--;
                if(j < 0)
                {
                    cout << j;
```

```
                    cout << "j is < 0\n";
                    break;
            }
        }
        while(m_rgl[j] > lKey);

        if(i < j)
        {
            // If the pointers did not cross that means there is a swap
            // required to place the two values in the correct partitions
            lT = m_rgl[i];
            m_rgl[i] = m_rgl[j];
            m_rgl[j] = lT;
        }
    }
    // Now the pointers crossed but the right most element is not in the
    // correct partition.
    // The ith element is also not in the correct partition. The right jth
    // element is.
    m_rgl[iRight] = m_rgl[i];
    m_rgl[i] = lKey;
    QuickSort(iLeft, i-1);
    QuickSort(i+1, iRight);
}
// This partition all sorted
}


void SArray::Sort(sortMethod sm)
{
    switch(sm)
    {
    case sortQuick:
        QuickSort(0, m_clMac-1);
        break;
    default:
        break;
    }
}




long g_rgl1[] = {20, 10, 5, 21, 32, 1};
long g_rgl2[] = {1, 2, 3, 4, 5, 6};
long g_rgl3[] = {5, 4, 3, 2, 1, 0};
```

```
void TestBSrch(long *rgl, int cl)
{
    SArray sa;
    long lMax = 0;
    int i;

    for(i=0; i<cl;i++)
    {
        if(rgl[i] > lMax)
            lMax = rgl[i];
        sa.IndexInsert(rgl[i]);
    }
    sa.Dump();
    for(i=0;i<lMax+2;i++)
    {
        cout << sa.IndexFind(i);
        cout << " ";
    }
    cout << '\n';
}

void TestSort(long *rgl, int cl)
{
    SArray sa;
    long lMax = 0;
    int i;

    for(i=0; i<cl;i++)
    {
        if(rgl[i] > lMax)
            lMax = rgl[i];
        sa.UnsortedInsert(rgl[i]);
        }
        cout << "before sorting : ";
        sa.Dump();
        sa.Sort(sortQuick);
        cout << "after sorting : ";
    sa.Dump();
    for(i=0;i<lMax+2;i++)
    {
        cout << sa.IndexFind(i);
        cout << " ";
    }
    cout << '\n';
}
```

```
int main(int argc, char *argv[])
{
    TestBSrch(g_rgl1, (sizeof(g_rgl1)/sizeof(long)));
    TestSort(g_rgl1, (sizeof(g_rgl1)/sizeof(long)));
    TestBSrch(g_rgl2, (sizeof(g_rgl2)/sizeof(long)));
    TestSort(g_rgl2, (sizeof(g_rgl2)/sizeof(long)));
    TestBSrch(g_rgl3, (sizeof(g_rgl3)/sizeof(long)));
    TestSort(g_rgl3, (sizeof(g_rgl3)/sizeof(long)));
    return 0;
}
```

CHAPTER 23
Regular Expression Matching

REGULAR EXPRESSION MATCHING IS ONE OF OUR FAVORITE EXAMPLES because it is chock-full of techniques. Regular expression matching provides a powerful way to examine strings. Instead of looking for exact matches, such as "Is the value of the string foo" or even "Does the string contain the substring foo," regular expression matching lets you find patterns. For example, you could look for strings that start with f or strings that start with f and then contain a sequence of one or more bar substrings. You can look for very sophisticated patterns.

Using the regular expression code, you can see if a string matches a pattern. You define a pattern by including special characters within a string. To do so, enter \\, followed by one of the following:

d	Matches any digit
D	Fails if there is any digit
w	Matches any letter (a–z, A–Z) or number
W	Fails if there is any letter or number
s	Matches any white space (spaces, tabs, returns, etc.)
S	Fails if there is any white space

For example, the following text will match any strings that start with this, followed, in order, by white space, is, white space, a, white space, and finally, by test1:

```
Literal li("this\\sis\\sa\\stest1");
```

Files

Here are the actual source code listings for the regular expression matching files. The header file is regexp.h, and the code file is regexp.cpp. The technique numbers in the comments refer to techniques in Part I. You can find these files and a corresponding Visual C++ project file in the exp folder on this book's accompanying CD-ROM.

regexp.h

```
#ifndef _REGEXP_H
#define _REGEXP_H
#include <typeinfo.h>
#include <string.h>

void TestRegExp();
// Repeat Info
typedef enum
{
   riOnce,
   riOneOrMore,
   riZeroOrMore,
   riMinMax,
}RI;



// Maximum any operator can repeat
const DWORD cdwMaxRI=0xfff;

class RExp
{
private:
   DWORD m_ri:3;
   DWORD m_cdwMin:12;
   DWORD m_cdwMax:12;
protected:
   static BOOL FIsWhiteRExp(char ch)
   {
      return (ch == '\n' || ch == '\r' || ch == '\f' || ch == '\t' ||
        ch == ' ');
   }

   int IChInSz(unsigned char ch, const char *pch, int cch);

   BOOL FInRangeRExp(char ch, char chMin, char chLast)
   {
      return (ch >= chMin && ch <= chLast);
   }
```

```
    BOOL FIsDigitRExp(char ch)
    {
       return FInRangeRExp(ch, '0', '9');
    }

    BOOL FIsWordCharRExp(char ch)
    {
       return FInRangeRExp(ch, 'a', 'z') || FInRangeRExp(ch, 'A', 'Z') ||
   FInRangeRExp(ch, '0', '9');
    }

    BOOL FSpecialChar(char chToken, char chSrc);
    // Is the token at the beginning of the szSrc. Returns -1 if it's not. Else it
    // returns the number of characters of the token string.
    int IStartTokenPchOnce(const char *szSrc, char *szToken);
    int IStartTokenPch(const char *szSrc, char *szToken);
public:
    RExp(DWORD cdwMin=1, DWORD cdwMax=1) : m_cdwMin(cdwMin), m_cdwMax(cdwMax),
   m_ri(riOnce)
    {
    }

    virtual ~RExp()
    {
    }

    RI  RiValue(void)
    {
       return (RI)m_ri;
    }

    void SetRi(RI ri)
    {
       switch(ri)
       {
       case riMinMax:
          return;
       case riOnce:
          m_cdwMin = 1;
          m_cdwMax = 1;
          break;
```

```
            case riZeroOrMore:
                m_cdwMin = 0;
                m_cdwMax = cdwMaxRI;
                break;
            case riOneOrMore:
                m_cdwMin = 1;
                m_cdwMax = cdwMaxRI;
                break;
        }
        m_ri = ri;
    }


    DWORD CMin(void)
    {
        return m_cdwMin;
    }


    DWORD CMax(void)
    {
        return m_cdwMax;
    }


    void SetCMinMax(DWORD cdwMin, DWORD cdwMax)
    {
        m_ri = riMinMax;
        // Some boundary checks. This is because we use bit fields. But it's a small
        // price to pay for the benefit of storing the information in less space.
        if(cdwMin > cdwMaxRI)
            cdwMin = cdwMaxRI;
        if(cdwMax < cdwMin)
            cdwMax = cdwMin;

        m_cdwMin = cdwMin;
        m_cdwMax = cdwMax;
    }


    // Search the string pch and returns the index at which the string match ends
    virtual int IMatch(const char *pch) = 0;
};

const cchLiteral = 256;
const cchCl = 255;
```

```
class Literal : public RExp
{
private:
    char m_rgch[cchLiteral];
public:
    Literal(const char *sz = NULL) : RExp()
    {
        if(sz)
        {
            strncpy(m_rgch, sz, sizeof(m_rgch)-2);
            m_rgch[sizeof(m_rgch) - 1] = 0;
        }
        else
            m_rgch[0] = 0;
    }

    const Literal &operator=(const Literal &literal)
    {
        if(&literal != this)
        {
            strcpy(m_rgch, literal.m_rgch);
        }
        return *this;
    }

    const Literal &operator=(const char *pch)
    {
        // Technique 42
        // Technique 43
        // Technique 61
        strncpy(m_rgch, pch, sizeof(m_rgch)-2);

        // Technique 41
        m_rgch[sizeof(m_rgch) - 1] = 0;
        return *this;
    }

    const Literal & operator+=(const char *sz)
    {
        int cchSrc;

        cchSrc = strlen(m_rgch);
        // +1 means there is enough space with the null terminator.
```

```
        // +2 means there is space to insert another character and then null
        // terminator.
        if(cchSrc+strlen(sz) + 1 < sizeof(m_rgch))
        {
            strcpy(m_rgch+cchSrc, sz);
        }
        return *this;
    }


    int IMatch(const char *pch)
    {
        return IStartTokenPch(pch, m_rgch);
    }
};

class Cl : public RExp
{
private:
    char m_rgch[cchCl];
    BOOL m_fContain:7;
    BOOL m_fSpecial:1;


public:
    Cl(const char *sz = NULL) : RExp(), m_fContain(TRUE), m_fSpecial(FALSE)
    {
        if(sz)
        {
            SetSz(sz);
        }
        else
            m_rgch[0] = 0;
    }

    void SetSz(const char *sz)
    {
        int cchDst;
        cchDst = strlen(sz);
        if(IChInSz('\\', sz, cchDst) >= 0 || IChInSz('-', sz, cchDst) >= 0)
            m_fSpecial = TRUE;
        else
            m_fSpecial = FALSE;
        strncpy(m_rgch, sz, sizeof(m_rgch)-2);
        m_rgch[sizeof(m_rgch) - 1] = 0;
    }
```

```
const Cl &operator=(const Cl &cl)
{
    if(&cl != this)
    {
        SetSz(cl.m_rgch);
    }
    return *this;
}


const Cl &operator=(const char *pch)
{
    SetSz(pch);
    return *this;
}

const Cl & operator+=(char *sz)
{
    int cchSrc;
    int cchDst;

    cchSrc = strlen(m_rgch);
    // +1 means there is enough space with the null terminator.
    if(cchSrc+(cchDst = strlen(sz)) + 1 < sizeof(m_rgch))
    {
        if(!m_fSpecial)
        {
            if(IChInSz('\\', sz, cchDst) >= 0 || IChInSz('-', sz, cchDst) >= 0)
                    m_fSpecial = TRUE;
        }
        strcpy(m_rgch+cchSrc, sz);
    }
    return *this;
}

void Contain(BOOL fContain)
{
    m_fContain = fContain;
}

int FMatch(const char *pch)
{
    char *pchToken;
    char chToken;
    char chSrc = *pch;
```

```
        // If there are no special characters, then use the faster comparison
        if(!m_fSpecial)
        {
            int ich;
            ich = IChInSz(chSrc, m_rgch, strlen(m_rgch));
            if(m_fContain)
                return ich >= 0;
            else
                return ich < 0;
        }

        pchToken = m_rgch;
        while(chToken = *pchToken++)
        {
            if('\\' == chToken)
            {
                if(FSpecialChar(*pchToken, chSrc))
                    return m_fContain;
                pchToken++;
            }
            else
            {
                char chTokenNext;
                if((chTokenNext = *pchToken) && '-' == chTokenNext)
                {
                    pchToken++;
                    if(FInRangeRExp(chSrc, chToken, *pchToken++))
                        return m_fContain;
                }
                if(chToken == chSrc)
                    return m_fContain;
            }
        }
        return !m_fContain;
    }

    int IMatch(const char *pch)
    {
        if(FMatch(pch))
            return 1;
        return -1;
    }
};
#endif _REGEXP_H
```

regexp.cpp

```cpp
#include <iostream.h>
#include "drg.h"
#include "stack.h"
#include "regexp.h"

// Technique 82
class FixedSize
{
    DWORD dwRes1:4;
    DWORD dwRes2:4;
    DWORD fRes3:1;
    DWORD fRes4:1;
    DWORD dwUnused:22;
};
#ifdef _DEBUG
char szFixedSizeAssert[sizeof(DWORD)-sizeof(FixedSize)+1];
#endif //DEBUG



// Technique 131
// Technique 132
// Technique 133
// Technique 134
// Technique 135

#pragma warning( disable : 4035 )
// return - 1 if the ch is not in pch else return the index of the matched
// character.
int RExp::IChInSz(unsigned char chSrc, const char *pch, int cch)
{
_asm
    {
    xor eax, eax
    mov al, chSrc
    mov edi, pch
    mov ecx, cch
    cld
    repnz scasb
    jz Found
    xor eax, eax
    jmp End
```

```
Found:
    mov eax, cch      ; cch - cchFound gives us the exact character since scasb
                      ; decrements the count before checking for the value.
    sub eax, ecx
End:
    dec eax           ; Since we need to return the index, subtract 1 from the
                      ; number of characters scanned

    }
}
#pragma warning( default : 4035 )

BOOL RExp::FSpecialChar(char chToken, char chSrc)
{
    switch(chToken)
    {
    case 'd':
        return FIsDigitRExp(chSrc);
    case 'D':
        return !FIsDigitRExp(chSrc);
    case 'w':
        return FIsWordCharRExp(chSrc);
    case 'W':
        return !FIsWordCharRExp(chSrc);
    case 's':
        return FIsWhiteRExp(chSrc);
    case 'S':
        return !FIsWhiteRExp(chSrc);
    default:
        return (chToken == chSrc);
    }
}

// Is the token at the beginning of the szSrc? Returns -1 if it's not. Else it
// returns the number of characters of the token string.
int RExp::IStartTokenPchOnce(const char *szSrc, char *szToken)
{
    char *pchToken = szToken;
    const char *pchSrc = szSrc;
    char chToken;
    char chSrc;
```

```
    while(TRUE)
    {
        // If the token string is completed we have a match.
        if(0 == (chToken = *pchToken))
            return pchSrc - szSrc;
        // If the source string is completed we don't have a match.
        if(0 == (chSrc = *pchSrc))
            return -1;

        if(chToken == '\\')
        {
            pchToken++;
            if(!FSpecialChar(*pchToken, chSrc))
                return -1;
        }
        else
        {
            if(chSrc != chToken)
                return -1;
        }
        pchSrc++;
        pchToken++;
    }
}


int RExp::IStartTokenPch(const char *szSrc, char *szToken)
{
    int iMatchT;
    const char *pch = szSrc;
    DWORD cdwMin;
    DWORD cdwMax;


    cdwMin = m_cdwMin;
    cdwMax = m_cdwMax;
    while(cdwMin >0)
    {
        iMatchT = IStartTokenPchOnce(pch, szToken);
        // Has to match minimum cdwMin times. If not return no match.
        if(iMatchT < 0)
            return 0;
        pch += iMatchT;
        --cdwMin;
        --cdwMax;
    }
```

```
        while(cdwMax >0)
        {
                iMatchT = IStartTokenPchOnce(pch, szToken);
                if(iMatchT < 0)
                    return pch - szSrc;
                pch += iMatchT;
                --cdwMax;
        }
        return pch - szSrc;
}


void TestRegExp()
{

    // Technique 38
    Literal li("this\\sis\\sa\\stest1");
    Cl  cl("p-u\\de-i0-7");
    Cl  cl1("this");

    // Technique 76
    const type_info& t = typeid(&li);
    cout << '\n' << t.name() << '\n' << t.raw_name() << '\n';

    cout << "Match results are" << li.IMatch("this is a test1 plus something
    else") << '\n';
    cout << "Match results for t38h are" << cl.IMatch("t") << ' ' <<
    cl.IMatch("3") << ' ' << cl.IMatch("8") << ' ' << cl.IMatch("h") << '\n';
    cout << "Match results for this are" << cl1.IMatch("t") << ' ' <<
    cl1.IMatch("h") << ' ' << cl1.IMatch("i") << ' ' << cl1.IMatch("s") << '\n';
    cout << "Match results for abc1 are" << cl1.IMatch("a") << ' ' <<
    cl1.IMatch("b") << ' ' << cl1.IMatch("c") << ' ' << cl1.IMatch("1") << '\n';
}
```

About the CD-ROM

THE COMPANION CD-ROM FOR this book is readable on Windows 95, 98, and NT 3.5 or later operating systems. This appendix tells you what you'll find on the CD and a little bit about how to use it.

Loading the CD Contents

After inserting the CD-ROM into the appropriate drive, you must manually copy the contents from the CD-ROM onto your local hard drive. The copying can be done through Explorer, File Manager, or from the command line. (Or you can just leave the files on the CD-ROM and look at them there. But if you want to edit them or compile them, you must copy them to your hard drive.)

With Explorer or File Manager, just drag the contents from the *Samples* directory on the CD-ROM to wherever you want to install it.

To use the contents of the CD, you must have a system that is capable of running Visual C++ 6.0. You should also have Visual C++ 6.0 installed on your machine. Of course, if all you want to do is look at the files, but not compile or run them, you can just use Notepad or any other text editor of your choice.

What's on the CD?

The CD-ROM contains all the source code and associated project files from the programming examples in this book.

You can also find the code from this book on www.essentialtechniques.com. From time to time, we'll also put updates or new samples there.

If You Have Any CD Problems

For technical support on using the CD, please send an e-mail message to support@apress.com. Your e-mail should include the nature of your problem or question, what operating system you are running, and what Visual C++ version you are using; finally, please be sure to tell us the best way to contact you. (No need to tell us your favorite color.)

Index

0, dividing by, 17–18
0, mod'ing with, 18
1-3-5 rule, 6
4035 warning, 149–150

A

abstract base classes, 83–91
    designing, 86–87
    inheritance from, 111
    instantiation of, 83–85, 87
    multiple inheritance in, 89–91
    purpose of, 83
    vtables and, 88
    See also base classes; classes; derived
        classes
access modifiers for inheritance, 110–111
access violations, 81, 159
access.cpp (reference counting source code
    file), 176–178
accessor functions, 65
accuracy versus execution speed, 139
Add method, 175
advice, programming. *See* programming
    advice
algorithms
    effect on performance, 133
    instead of assembly language, 12
    manipulating bit fields in, 199
    selecting, 11–12
    sorting, 207
aliasing with references, 132
allocated data, pointers to, 118
allocating
    arrays, 55, 76
    buffers, 45–46, 48
    nonstatic consts, 63–64
allocating memory. *See* memory allocations
ANSI string class, 191
Append function, 41
applications, testing multiple, 155
arguments
    for const operators, 72–74
    validating, 15–16

arithmetics
    floating point versus integer on a
        Pentium, 137
    logical operators in, 159
arrays, 55–58
    allocating, 55, 76
    compiler adjustments of, 21
    defined, 55
    deleting, 55
    dereferencing elements, 56, 57
    dynamic, 179–189
    foo[K], same as foo.operator[ ](K), 57–58
    index notations for, 58
    index overflows and underflows,
        avoiding, 55–57
    initializing, 47–48
    look-up tables for, 139
    look-ups versus pointer arithmetic,
        142–144
    as pointers, 58
    reallocating, 179
    versus data structures, 11–12, 55
assembly language, 147–150
    algorithms instead of, 12
    C++ variables, accessing, 147–148
    debugging, 153, 162, 167
    inline assembly for specific processors, 148
    #pragmas, 150
    restoring warning defaults after
        disabling, 150
    setting eax, 148–150
    See also compiler-generated code
asserts
    code comments and, 24–25
    for guarding assumptions, 17
    missing from retail builds, 25–26
    for uncovering memory problems, 45, 54
automatic variables, returning pointers to,
    46–47

B

backslashes in strings, use of, 31
base address collisions, avoiding, 136

227

E

EAX registers, 148–150, 159
EBP registers, 159, 165, 166, 167
ECX registers, 159, 165, 166
edge cases, 33
edge conditions, testing under, 154
EDI registers, 159
EDX registers, 159
EIP registers, 23, 159, 161, 162
elements in arrays
    dereferencing, 56
    setting numbers for, 76
embedding classes, and delegating to, 75
encapsulation of member variables, 65
= operators
    in C++, 19–20
    overloading, 116–118, 180
    overriding when allocating memory,
        68–69, 97–99
equality comparisons, 19–20
errors
    syntax, 58
    using const const, 50–51
    using smart pointers, 52
    warnings treated as, 29–30
escape characters (backslashes), using in
        strings, 31
ESI registers, 23, 159
E_SITENOTFOUND, 23
ESP registers, 159
even and odd numbers, role in debugging, 167
exceptions
    first-chance, 160
    handling, 25–26
executables, loading for debugging, 157–158
execution
    skipping during debugging, 161
    speed versus accuracy of, 139
expanding arrays, 179
expressions
    #define in, 29
    source code listing for expression
        matching, 213–224
    writing, 141

F

failure of memory allocations, 45
features of products, defining, 6
feedback from customers, 9
FGrow method for dynamic arrays, 180

file access, speed of, 133
file paths, checking, 128
files for source code listings
    access.cpp (reference counting),
        176–178
    bits.cpp (bit manipulation), 200–206
    bsrch.cpp (sorting), 207–212
    drg.cpp (dynamic arrays), 184–189
    drg.h (dynamic arrays), 181–184
    regexp.cpp (regular expression
        matching), 221–224
    regexp.h (regular expression matching),
        214–220
    smartptr.cpp (smart pointers), 173–174
    smartptr.h (smart pointers), 172–173
    string.cpp (strings), 192–198
files, wrapping headers with sentinels, 20–21
first-chance exceptions, 160
float type intrinsics, 118
floating point versus integer math on a
        Pentium, 137
freeing memory, 44, 51–52, 171
function calls, extra, 40
functions, 118
    of base classes, 74–75
    behavior of, 32–33
    copying, 14
    inline, 136
fundamental algorithms, 199

G

general protection (GP) faults, 64
generalizing design, 9, 11
GIF graphics in RC files, 127
global memory allocators, 54
global nonstatic consts, 63–64
good design, importance of, 8–9
GP (general protection) faults, 64
graphic file resources, inserting, 127
guarding assumptions, 17

H

.h files, problems with, 20–21
handles, creating, 144
hardware breakpoints, 161
HasA versus IsA relationships, 107–108
header file paths, checking, 128
header files, wrapping with sentinels, 20–21

O

P

Q

R

S

Apress™

License Agreement (Single-User Products)

THIS IS A LEGAL AGREEMENT BETWEEN YOU, THE END USER, AND APRESS. BY OPENING THE SEALED DISK PACK-AGE, YOU ARE AGREEING TO BE BOUND BY THE TERMS OF THIS AGREEMENT. IF YOU DO NOT AGREE TO THE TERMS OF THIS AGREEMENT, PROMPTLY RETURN THE UNOPENED DISK PACKAGE AND THE ACCOMPANYING ITEMS (IN-CLUDING WRITTEN MATERIALS AND BINDERS AND OTHER CONTAINERS) TO THE PLACE YOU OBTAINED THEM FOR A FULL REFUND.

APRESS SOFTWARE LICENSE

1. GRANT OF LICENSE. APress grants you the right to use one copy of this enclosed APress software program (the "SOFT-WARE") on a single terminal connected to a single computer (i.e., with a single CPU). You may not network the SOFTWARE or otherwise use it on more than one computer or computer terminal at the same time.

2. COPYRIGHT. The SOFTWARE copyright is owned by APress or its suppliers and is protected by United States copyright laws and international treaty provisions. Therefore, you must treat the SOFTWARE like any other copyrighted material (e.g., a book or musical recording) except that you may either (a) make one copy of the SOFTWARE solely for backup or archival purposes, or (b) transfer the SOFTWARE to a single hard disk, provided you keep the original solely for backup or archival purposes. You may not copy the written material accompanying the SOFTWARE.

3. OTHER RESTRICTIONS. You may not rent or lease the SOFTWARE, but you may transfer the SOFTWARE and accompa-nying written materials on a permanent basis provided you retain no copies and the recipient agrees to the terms of this Agreement. You may not reverse engineer, decompile, or disassemble the SOFTWARE. If SOFTWARE is an update, any transfer must include the update and all prior versions.

4. DUAL MEDIA SOFTWARE. If the SOFTWARE package contains both 3.5″ and 5.25″ disks, then you may use only the disks appropriate for your single-user computer. You may not use the other disks on another computer or loan, rent, lease, or transfer them to another user except as part of the permanent transfer (as provided above) of all SOFTWARE and writ-ten materials.

LIMITED WARRANTY

LIMITED WARRANTY. APress warrants that the SOFTWARE will perform substantially in accordance with the accompany-ing written material for a period of 90 days from the receipt. Any implied warranties on the SOFTWARE are limited to 90 days. Some states do not allow limitations on duration of an implied warranty, so the above limitation may not apply to you.

CUTOMER REMEDIES. APress's entire liability and your exclusive remedy shall be, at APress's option, either (a) return of the price paid or (b) repair or replacement of the SOFTWARE that does not meet APress's Limited Warranty and which is returned to APress with a copy of your receipt. This limited warranty is void if failure of the SOFTWARE has resulted from accident, abuse, or misapplication. Any replacement SOFTWARE will be warranted for the remainder of the original war-ranty period or 30 days, whichever is longer. These remedies are not available outside of the United States of America.

NO OTHER WARRANTIES. APress disclaims all other warranties, either express or implied, including but not limited to im-plied warranties of merchantability and fitness for a particular purpose, with respect to the SOFTWARE and the accompa-nying written materials. This limited warranty gives you specific rights. You may have others, which vary from state to state.

NO LIABILITIES FOR CONSEQUENTIAL DAMAGES. In no event shall APress or its suppliers be liable for any damages whatsoever (including, without limitation, damages from loss of business profits, business interruption, loss of business information, or other pecuniary loss) arising out of the use or inability to use this APress product, even if APress has been advised of the possibility of such damages. Because some states do not allow the exclusion or limitation of liability for con-sequential or incidental damages, the above limitation may not apply to you.

U.S. GOVERNMENT RESTRICTED RIGHTS

The SOFTWARE and documentation are provided with RESTRICTED RIGHTS. Use, duplication, or disclosure by the Gov-ernment is subject to restriction as set forth in subparagraph (c)(1)(ii) of The Rights in Technical Data and Computer Soft-ware clause at 52.227-7013. Contractor/manufacturer is APress, 6400 Hollis Street, Suite 9, Emeryville, CA 94608.

This Agreement is governed by the laws of the State of California.

Should you have any questions concerning this Agreement, or if you wish to contact APress for any reason, please write to APress, 6400 Hollis Street, Suite 9, Emeryville, CA 94608.